The Complete Lean and Green Cookbook for Beginners

1500+ Days of Fueling Hacks & Green Tasty Recipes. Reach a Healthy and Fit Life Permanently by Harnessing the Power of "Fueling Hacks Meals"

Rosalinda Sherman

Table of Contents

Introduction

The foundations of the Lean and Green Diet

The Lean & Green Diet encourages living a healthy, environmentally friendly lifestyle. The Diet comprises exercising regularly, consuming less animal products, using fewer fossil fuels, and leading a sustainable lifestyle. This diet can help you live a longer, healthier life by allowing you to personally make decisions about your health rather than depending on external pressures like businesses or lobbyists to influence your choices.

The Lean & Green Diet is becoming increasingly popular due to it many positive health effects, including a higher intake of fruits and vegetables - at least two portions each day, along with one piece of lean protein like chicken, fish, or poultry, are often included in this diet. Lean protein and a concentration on plant-based meals can help you lose weight and enhance your health in general.

The Lean & Green Diet is a weight reduction plan that attempts to assist you in losing weight and helping you keep it off permanently. It places a strong emphasis on portion management, wholesome meals, avoiding processed foods, and regular exercise to help you attain a healthy physique with the least amount of effort. Lean meats, vegetables, fruits, nuts, seeds, and whole grains are all included in the diet, which has been found to improve weight and general health, including lowering the risk of developing cancer. By encouraging you to spend time outside and exercise, the Lean & Green Diet may also give you more energy and lift your spirits.

The Lean & Green Diet does not support this strategy since it understands that completely cutting out some meals might be harmful to the digestive system. Instead, it places a focus on the consumption of low-fat, high-protein lean meats. The diet emphasizes the usage of lean protein sources, which have less fat than red flesh and may aid in weight loss. Examples include fish, chicken breasts, and beefsteak. The diet suggests eggs for breakfast since they are a wonderful source of healthy fats that can boost your protein consumption. The diet advises include seafood in your meal, such as salmon and sardines, to lower saturated fats. The Lean & Green Diet recommends consuming 1- 2 portions of meat per day, or more than 6 ounces per day for individuals who exercise often.

The Lean & Green Diet encourages eating a lot of veggies since they are low in fat yet high in essential vitamins and minerals. The usage of nuts, seeds, and vegetable oils like olive oil as sources of healthy fats is also encouraged. Numerous benefits of this diet are said to include weight loss, decreased blood pressure and cholesterol, and improved cognitive function. Particularly low in calories and rich in minerals like calcium, iron, magnesium, and vitamin C are green vegetables.

The Lean & Green Diet seeks to encourage weight reduction without impairing the body's natural metabolic functions, improving digestive health, and increasing metabolic rate. The diet represents a nutritious, well-balanced eating regimen that may lengthen life by lowering the risk of a variety of diseases, including cancer, heart disease, and stroke. Additionally, it could be a sensible financial decision for those that prioritize their health.

For their ability to aid in weight loss, lean protein sources with minimal fat content, especially those with little to no saturated fat, are given preference in the diet. The regimen also contains a variety of fruits and vegetables in addition to lean protein in order to provide a variety of nutrients and support general health.

The Lean & Green Diet encourages human health and environmental responsibility by avoiding factory-farmed beef that could be treated with hormones or steroids, or produced in an inhumane manner. Instead, the diet advocates buying meat from free-range farms that don't use antibiotics or chemical treatments on their livestock. If you want to increase your protein consumption without increasing saturated fat, the plan suggests choosing lean options like chicken breasts and grass-fed beef. Along with meat, the diet recommends a variety of fruits and vegetables, as well as protein from eggs, fish, shellfish, and other seafood. The Lean & Green Diet places more of an emphasis on whole, natural ingredients than it does on processed foods, which may include fungicides and chemical additives.

The foundation of the Lean & Green Diet is the notion that our bodies typically only store energy for a little amount of time before requiring more. We educate our body to have limited energy and to show hunger signals earlier by eating smaller meals and snacks in between them, which makes us feel like we need to eat more to sustain ourselves. Because of this, even after eating lately, we could still feel hungry. However, because they don't feel the same hunger cues, those who eat three meals a day often consume fewer calories overall. Even when eating foods that are low in fat or calories, such salads and vegetables, it's crucial to be conscious of the sorts of food we eat when on a low-calorie diet.

The Lean & Green Diet suggests the following methods for consuming less fat and selecting healthier options:
1. Choose vinaigrette dressings over ranch dressings, which are rich in saturated fat, and mayonnaise-based dressings.
2. Steer clear of deep-fried dishes because they contain the most fat and instead consider sautéing veggies.
3. Avoid fried meat and go for grilled or broiled meat.
4. Choose delicate or tomato-based gravies over cream gravies, which are heavy in fat.
5. To keep track of fat intake, check the nutrition information marked on food packaging.
6. Choose reduced- fat or low- fat cheeses rather of full- fat ones.
7. Limit consumption of processed flesh like ham and salami, which can be high in salt and preservatives.
8. Avoid fried dishes like French fries, which are cooked in oil painting or grease and have a high saturated fat content.
9. Limit red meat input to two servings per week and choose grilling or roasting cooking styles over frying.
10. Opt for low-fat dairy products like skim and 1% milk, cheeses, yogurt, and sour cream.

The Lean & Green Diet is a plant-based diet with a focus on lean meat wherever feasible, vegetables and grains, legumes, nuts and seeds (like almonds), and non-dairy milk. Lean meats are included as they can provide protein without adding extra fat or carbs. The diet features aspects of the raw, vegetarian, vegan, and vegetarian cuisines. Vegetables are an essential component of the regime, containing a range of foods such potatoes, onions, peppers, broccoli, celery, and cauliflower. These are also abundant in minerals, vitamins, fiber, and antioxidants. Another crucial component of the diet is fruit, as a source of vitamins and minerals that support cardiovascular health. In addition to veggies and fruits, the diet also includes a range of fiber-rich grains to help you feel satiated for longer.

The meal plans

When following the Lean & Green Diet or any weight reduction strategy, it's crucial to take into account not just what and when you consume, but also how frequently. The dietary habits and tastes of each individual vary, so what works for one person might not work for another. Others like fewer, more frequent meals, while some prefer to have one substantial meal each day and skip or only have a little snack for lunch. Instead of relying on harmful habits like binge eating or skipping meals, it's critical to create a balance that works for you and matches your lifestyle. In addition to the sorts of meals you select and when you consume them, it's crucial to take into account your eating frequency because it might affect your general health and weight control goals. Individual eating patterns and tastes might differ widely, with some people favoring diets high in carbs, sugar, adipose-storing meals, or plant-based foods. People may need to adapt their routines and adjust their eating habits in order to follow the Lean & Green Diet. In addition to one, two, or three main meals throughout the day, this diet stresses "fueling" the body with frequent, smaller meals.

The Lean & Green Diet is a good option for many people due to its adaptability and practicality. It is advised to test out several strategies to see which one suits you and your objectives the best. A cookbook with wholesome, well-balanced dishes can also aid with diet maintenance. Depending on whatever version of the Lean & Green Diet you follow, eating six to seven times a day is advised.

Five "fuelings" (smaller meals) are included in the **Optimal Weight 5 & 1 Plan** each day, along with one balanced lean and green meal. The **Optimal Weight 4 & 2 & 1** Plan consists of four fuelings, two lean and green meals, and one snack per day and is intended for persons who require more calories and flexibility in their dietary choices. The **Optimal Health 3 & 3 Plan**, which comprises three fuelings and three balanced lean and green meals each day, is designed for maintenance. These dietary guidelines for meal frequency are meant to aid in maintaining a healthy weight and body composition.

Chapter 1: Breakfast Recipes

Peanut Butter Yogurt Dip with Fruit

Prep Time: 5 minutes, **Serving:** 4

Ingredients:

- 1 cup plain Greek yogurt
- 2 tablespoons peanut butter
- 1 tablespoon honey
- 1 teaspoon vanilla extract
- Assorted fruit, such as sliced apples, berries, and bananas, for dipping

Directions:

1. In a small mixing bowl, stir together the yogurt, peanut butter, honey, and vanilla extract until smooth.
2. Serve the peanut butter yogurt dip with a selection of your favorite fruit for dipping. Enjoy!

Nutrition (per serving): Fat: 13g, Net Carbs: 18g, Protein: 9g, Sodium: 65mg

Mushroom Spinach Egg Muffins

Prep Time: 10 minutes **Cook time:** 20 minutes **Serving:** 12 muffins

Ingredients:

- 10 large eggs
- 1/2 pound baby spinach
- 1/2 pint cherry or grape tomatoes
- 8 ounces feta cheese, crumbled
- 1/2 cup chopped mushrooms
- Butter or olive oil, as needed
- Salt & pepper, to taste

Directions:

1. Preheat your oven to 350°F (180°C). Grease a muffin tin with butter or olive oil.
2. In a large mixing bowl, beat the eggs until they are fully mixed.
3. In a skillet over medium heat, melt some butter or heat some olive oil. Add the mushrooms and cook for about 5 minutes, until they are tender.
4. Add the spinach to the skillet with the mushrooms and cook for an additional 7-10 minutes, until the spinach leaves are wilted.
5. Cut the cherry or grape tomatoes into small pieces.
6. Divide the spinach and mushroom mixture evenly among the muffin cups. Top each muffin cup with a sprinkle of feta cheese and some chopped cherry or grape tomatoes.
7. Pour the beaten eggs over the top of the spinach, mushrooms, cheese, and tomatoes in the muffin cups.
8. Bake the muffins for 20 minutes, or until they are set and golden brown on top.
9. Remove the muffins from the oven and let them cool for a few minutes before serving. Enjoy these healthy and delicious muffins as a breakfast or snack.

Nutrition (per muffin): Fat: 9g, Net Carbs: 4g, Protein: 7g, Sodium: 276mg

Egg Muffin

Prep Time: 10 minutes **Cook time:** 15-20 minutes **Serving:** 6

Ingredients:

- 6 large eggs
- 1/2 cup diced chicken breast
- 1/4 cup shredded cheese (low-fat)
- 1/2 cup diced bell pepper
- 1/4 cup diced onion
- 1/2 cup diced mushrooms
- Salt and pepper, to taste

Directions:

1. Preheat your oven to 350°F (180°C).
2. Crack the eggs into a large mixing bowl and whisk until fully combined.
3. Stir in the diced chicken breast, bell pepper, onion, mushrooms and season with salt and pepper.
4. Grease a muffin tin or line with muffin cups. Divide the egg mixture evenly among the cups.
5. Bake for 15-20 minutes, or until the eggs are fully cooked and the muffins are golden brown on top.
6. Serve hot and enjoy!

Nutrition (per serving): Calories: 140, Fat: 7g, Protein: 14g, Carbohydrates: 4g, Fiber: 1g

Baked Eggs

Prep Time: 10 minutes **Cook time:** 10 minutes **Serving:** 4

Ingredients:

- 10 large eggs
- 1/2 pound baby spinach
- 1/2 cup diced cherry or grape tomatoes
- 1/4 cup diced bell pepper
- 1/4 cup diced onion
- Salt and pepper, to taste

Directions:

1. Preheat your oven to 350°F (180°C).
2. Crack the eggs into a large mixing bowl and whisk until evenly combined.
3. Heat a pan over medium heat and add a bit of butter or olive oil. Pour the egg mixture into the pan and cook until the eggs are fully set, about 5-7 minutes.
4. Meanwhile, add another pan to the stove over medium heat and add a bit of butter or olive oil. Cook the spinach, bell pepper and onion for about 7-10 minutes until the spinach leaves are wilted and the vegetables are tender.
5. Once the eggs and spinach are cooked, place a portion of the cooked spinach and vegetables on a plate. Cut the eggs into small pieces and sprinkle them over the spinach.
6. Repeat this process with the remaining eggs, spinach and vegetables.
7. Serve with diced cherry or grape tomatoes on the side and enjoy!

Nutrition (per serving): Calories: 207, Fat: 15g, Protein: 17g, Carbohydrates: 4g, Fiber: 2g

Egg Avocado Toast

Ingredients:

- 4 slices of whole wheat bread
- 2 avocados, ripe
- 4 large eggs
- Salt and pepper, to taste
- 1/2 cup diced bell pepper
- 1/2 cup diced onion
- 1/2 cup diced mushrooms

Directions:

1. Preheat your oven to 425°F (220°C).
2. Place the bread on a baking sheet and toast in the preheated oven for 5-7 minutes, or until crispy.
3. Meanwhile, slice the avocados in half and remove the pits. Scoop the avocado flesh out of the skin and mash it in a small bowl using a fork.
4. Heat a small skillet over medium heat, add diced bell pepper, onion, mushrooms and cook for about 7-10 minutes until the vegetables are tender
5. Heat a small skillet over medium heat without oil. Crack the eggs into the skillet and sprinkle with salt and pepper. Cook the eggs until the whites are fully set, about 2-3 minutes per side.
6. Spread the mashed avocado evenly over the toasted bread slices. Top each slice with a cooked egg and the sauted vegetables
7. Serve immediately and enjoy the combination of creamy avocado and rich, yolky eggs on top of toasty bread and vegetables

Nutrition (per serving): Calories: 237, Fat: 17g, Carbohydrates: 20g, Protein: 11g, Fiber: 10g, Sodium: 184mg

Gingerbread Oatmeal Breakfast

Ingredients:

- Old fashioned oats
- 1/2 cup Water
- 1 cup Unsweetened almond milk
- 1/4 cup Ground ginger
- 1/2 tsp Ground cinnamon
- 1/4 tsp Ground cloves
- 1/4 tsp Ground nutmeg
- 1/4 tsp Stevia or erythritol
- 2 tbsp Chopped pecans or walnuts
- 1/2 cup Spinach or kale, finely chopped

Directions:

1. In a small saucepan, combine the oats, water, and almond milk. Bring the mixture to a boil over medium heat.

2. Reduce the heat to low and add in the ground ginger, cinnamon, cloves, and nutmeg. Stir to combine.
3. Add the finely chopped spinach or kale and stir to combine.
4. Let the oatmeal simmer for 5-7 minutes, or until it reaches your desired thickness.
5. Stir in the stevia or erythritol and top with the chopped nuts.
6. Serve hot and enjoy your delicious gingerbread oatmeal breakfast!

Nutrition: Fat: 4g, Net Carbs: 16g, Protein: 8g, Fiber: 4g, Sodium: 35mg

Avocado Toast with Radish

Prep Time: 5 minutes **Cook time:** 5 minutes **Serving:** 2

Ingredients:
- Sourdough bread
- 2 slices Avocado
- 1 Radish, 3-4 Lemon juice
- 1 tsp Olive oil
- 1 tbsp Salt
- to taste Pepper, to taste

Directions:
1. Toast the bread until it is crispy and golden brown.
2. In the meantime, slice the avocado and radish into thin pieces.
3. Squeeze the lemon juice over the avocado slices and mash them lightly with a fork.
4. Once the bread is toasted, spread the mashed avocado over the top of each slice.
5. Arrange the radish slices on top of the avocado.
6. Drizzle olive oil over the top and sprinkle with salt and pepper to taste.
7. Serve immediately and enjoy your delicious avocado toast with radish!

Nutrition (per serving): Fat: 15g, Net Carbs: 28g, Protein: 6g, Sodium: 200mg

Cheese Almond Pancakes

Prep Time: 5 minutes **Cook time:** 15 minutes **Serving:** 4

Ingredients:
- 1 cup Whole wheat flour
- 2 tsp Baking powder
- 1 tsp Salt
- 1/4 tsp Stevia or other low-calorie sweetener
- 2 tbsp Shredded low-fat cheese
- 1/2 cup Sliced almonds
- 1/2 cup Egg whites
- 1 cup Unsweetened almond milk
- 1 tbsp Olive oil

Directions:
1. In a medium mixing bowl, whisk together the whole wheat flour, baking powder, salt, and stevia.

2. Stir in the shredded cheese and sliced almonds.
3. In a separate bowl, whisk together the egg whites, almond milk, and olive oil.
4. Pour the wet ingredients into the dry ingredients and stir until just combined. Do not overmix.
5. Heat a large nonstick skillet over medium heat. Drop spoonfuls of the batter onto the skillet, using about 1/4 cup for each pancake.
6. Cook the pancakes for 2-3 minutes on each side, or until they are golden brown and cooked through.
7. Serve the pancakes warm, topped with low sugar syrup or fruit preserves. Enjoy your delicious cheese almond pancakes!

Nutrition (per serving): Fat: 12g, Net Carbs: 20g, Protein: 12g, Sodium: 240mg

Healthy Waffles

Prep Time: 10 minutes **Cook time:** 20 minutes **Serving:** 4

Ingredients:
- 1 1/2 cups whole wheat flour
- 2 tsp baking powder
- 1/2 tsp salt
- 2 eggs
- 2 tbsp almond milk
- 1 tsp vanilla extract
- 1/4 cup chopped fresh berries (blueberries, raspberries, strawberries)

Directions:
1. Preheat your waffle iron according to the manufacturer's instructions.
2. In a medium mixing bowl, whisk together the whole wheat flour, baking powder, and salt.
3. In a separate bowl, whisk together the eggs, almond milk, and vanilla extract.
4. Pour the wet ingredients into the dry ingredients and stir until just combined. Do not overmix.
5. Fold in the fresh berries.
6. Pour the batter into the preheated waffle iron, using about 1/2 cup for each waffle.
7. Close the waffle iron and cook the waffles for 5-7 minutes, or until they are golden brown and cooked through.
8. Serve the waffles warm, topped with more fresh berries and a drizzle of pure maple syrup. Enjoy your delicious and healthy waffles!

Nutrition (per serving): Fat: 11g, Net Carbs: 38g, Protein: 9g, Sodium: 230mg

Protein Muffins

Prep Time: 10 minutes **Cook time:** 20 minutes **Serving:** 12

Ingredients:
- 1 1/2 cups Protein powder (Whey or Plant based)
- 1/2 cup Baking powder
- 1 tsp Salt
- 1/2 tsp Eggs (or egg whites)

- 3 Stevia or monk fruit sweetener
- 1/3 cup Unsweetened applesauce
- 1/2 cup Almond milk
- 1 tsp Vanilla extract
- 1/2 cup Chopped spinach or kale (optional)

Directions:
1. Preheat your oven to 350°F (180°C). Line a muffin tin with paper liners or spray with cooking spray.
2. In a medium mixing bowl, whisk together the oats, protein powder, baking powder, and salt.
3. In a separate bowl, whisk together the eggs, sweetener, applesauce, almond milk, and vanilla extract.
4. Stir in the chopped spinach or kale, if using.
5. Pour the wet ingredients into the dry ingredients and stir until just combined.
6. Divide the batter evenly among the muffin cups, filling them about 3/4 full.
7. Bake the muffins for 18-20 minutes, or until a toothpick inserted in the center comes out clean.
8. Allow the muffins to cool for a few minutes before serving. Enjoy your delicious and protein-packed muffins!

Nutrition (per muffin): Fat: 4g, Net Carbs: 20g, Protein: 12g, Sodium: 180mg

Cold Banana Breakfast

Prep Time: 5 minutes **Cook time:** 0 minutes **Serving:** 1

Ingredients:
- 1 small banana
- 1 tbsp almond butter
- 1 tbsp chia seeds
- 1 tsp honey
- 1/4 cup unsweetened almond milk

Directions:
1. Slice the banana into rounds and set aside.
2. In a small bowl, mix together the almond butter, chia seeds, and honey.
3. Spread the almond butter mixture over the banana slices.
4. Pour the almond milk over the top and serve immediately. Enjoy your delicious cold banana breakfast!

Nutrition (per serving): Fat: 15g, Net Carbs: 27g, Protein: 4g, Sodium: 75mg

Strawberry Yogurt Treat

Prep Time: 10 minutes **Cook time:** 0 minutes **Serving:** 1

Ingredients:
- 1 cup plain, non-fat Greek yogurt
- 1 cup fresh or frozen strawberries
- 2 tbsp sweetener of your choice (such as stevia or monk fruit sweetener)

- 1 tsp granola (optional)

Directions:
1. In a small mixing bowl, stir together the Greek yogurt and sweetener until well combined.
2. Slice the strawberries into thin rounds and set aside.
3. To assemble the treat, place half of the yogurt mixture in the bottom of a small jar or bowl.
4. Top the yogurt with half of the sliced strawberries and a sprinkle of granola.
5. Repeat the layers with the remaining yogurt, strawberries, and granola.
6. Serve immediately or refrigerate until ready to eat.

Nutrition (per serving): Calories: 120, Fat: 0g, Net Carbs: 14g, Protein: 20g, Sodium: 70mg

Apple Oatmeal

Prep Time: 5 minutes **Cook time:** 15 minutes **Serving:** 2

Ingredients:
- 1 cup rolled oats
- 2 cups water
- 1 medium apple, peeled and diced
- 1 tsp cinnamon
- 1 tsp sweetener of your choice (such as stevia or monk fruit sweetener)
- 1/4 cup diced chicken breast or turkey breast (optional)

Directions:
1. Place the oats and water in a saucepan and bring to a boil over medium heat.
2. Once the oats and water are boiling, reduce the heat to low and add the diced apple and cinnamon.
3. Simmer the mixture, stirring occasionally, for 10-15 minutes or until the oats are cooked to your desired consistency.
4. Remove the saucepan from the heat and stir in the sweetener of your choice (if using).
5. Divide the oatmeal into bowls and top each bowl with diced chicken breast or turkey breast (if using).
6. Serve hot and enjoy!

Nutrition (per serving, with chicken breast or turkey breast): Calories: 250, Fat: 6g, Carbohydrates: 27g, Protein: 20g, Sodium: 55mg

Banana Cashew Toast

Prep Time: 5 minutes **Cook time:** 5 minutes **Serving:** 1

Ingredients:
- 1 slice whole wheat bread
- 1/2 medium banana, sliced
- 1 tbsp unsalted cashew butter
- 1 tsp sweetener of your choice (such as stevia or monk fruit sweetener)
- 1/4 cup diced chicken breast or turkey breast (optional)

Directions:
1. Toast the slice of bread to your desired level of doneness.
2. While the bread is toasting, mash the banana slices in a small bowl using a fork.

3. Once the bread is done toasting, spread the mashed banana on top of the toast.
4. Next, spread the cashew butter on top of the banana slices.
5. If desired, drizzle sweetener of your choice on top of the cashew butter.
6. Top the toast with diced chicken breast or turkey breast (if using)
7. Serve the toast immediately and enjoy!

Note: This recipe provides one serving of lean protein and one serving of healthy fat when using chicken breast or turkey breast. It should be paired with an additional serving of lean protein and healthy fat in order to meet the Lean&Green program guidelines.

Nutrition (per serving): Calories: 240, Fat: 12g, Carbohydrates: 31g, Protein: 7g, Sodium: 120mg

Cinnamon Pancakes with Coconut

Prep Time: 5 minutes **Cook time:** 10 minutes **Serving:** 4

Ingredients:
- 1/4 cup whole wheat flour
- 1/4 tsp baking powder
- 1/8 tsp salt
- 1/4 tsp ground cinnamon
- 1/4 cup unsweetened almond milk
- 1 egg white
- 1 tsp coconut oil, melted
- 1 tbsp shredded coconut
- 2 oz diced chicken breast or turkey breast (optional)

Directions:
1. In a medium bowl, whisk together the flour, baking powder, salt, and cinnamon.
2. In a separate small bowl, whisk together the almond milk and egg white.
3. Pour the wet ingredients into the dry ingredients and mix until just combined. Do not overmix.
4. Stir in the melted coconut oil and shredded coconut.
5. Heat a non-stick pan or griddle over medium heat.
6. Once hot, spoon 1/4 cup of the pancake batter onto the pan for each pancake.
7. Cook the pancakes for 1-2 minutes on each side, or until bubbles form on the surface and the edges start to look cooked.
8. Serve the pancakes hot with diced chicken breast or turkey breast (if using) as a lean protein option. Enjoy!

Nutrition (per serving, without diced chicken breast or turkey breast): Calories: 100, Fat: 5g, Carbohydrates: 12g, Protein: 3g, Sodium: 120mg.

Flaxseed Porridge with Cinnamon

Prep Time: 5 minutes **Cook time:** 10 minutes **Serving:** 1

Ingredients:
- 1/2 cup unsweetened almond milk
- 1/2 cup water
- 1/4 cup rolled oats
- 1 tbsp ground flaxseeds
- 1/2 tsp ground cinnamon
- 1/4 cup diced chicken breast or turkey breast (optional)

Directions:
1. Combine the almond milk, water, oats, flaxseeds, and cinnamon in a small saucepan.
2. Bring the mixture to a boil over medium heat, stirring occasionally.
3. Once boiling, reduce the heat to low and continue to cook the porridge for 5-7 minutes, or until it reaches your desired consistency.
4. Remove the saucepan from the heat and stir in diced chicken breast or turkey breast (if using).
5. Transfer the porridge to a bowl and serve hot. Enjoy!

Note: This recipe provides one serving of lean protein when using chicken breast or turkey breast. It should be paired with an additional serving of lean protein and healthy fat in order to meet the Lean&Green program guidelines.

Nutrition (per serving with chicken breast or turkey breast): Calories: 250, Fat: 4g, Carbohydrates: 22g, Protein: 20g, Sodium: 80mg

Pancake Cinnamon Buns

Prep Time: 5 minutes **Cook time:** 15 minutes **Serving:** 4

Ingredients:
- 1/2 cup whole wheat flour
- 1/2 cup oat flour
- 1 tsp baking powder
- 1/2 tsp salt
- 1/2 cup unsweetened almond milk
- 1 egg white
- 2 tbsp melted coconut oil, divided
- 1/4 cup diced chicken breast or turkey breast (optional)

Directions:
1. In a medium bowl, whisk together the whole wheat flour, oat flour, baking powder, and salt.
2. In a separate small bowl, whisk together the almond milk and egg white.
3. Pour the wet ingredients into the dry ingredients and mix until just combined. Do not overmix.
4. Heat a non-stick pan or griddle over medium heat. Once hot, spoon 1/4 cup of the pancake batter onto the pan for each bun.
5. Cook the buns for 1-2 minutes on each side, or until bubbles form on the surface and the edges start to look cooked.
6. While the buns are cooking, mix together the diced chicken breast or turkey breast (if using) with 1 tsp of cinnamon in a small bowl.
7. Once the buns are done cooking, top each bun with chicken breast or turkey breast mixture and drizzle with melted coconut oil.
8. Serve the buns hot and enjoy!

Nutrition (per serving, without chicken breast or turkey breast): Calories: 150, Fat: 8g, Carbohydrates: 17g, Protein: 4g, Sodium: 160mg

Pineapple Mango Pancakes

Prep Time: 5 minutes **Cook time:** 15 minutes **Serving:** 4

Ingredients:
- 1/2 cup almond flour
- 1/4 cup coconut flour

- 1 tsp baking powder
- 1/2 tsp salt
- 1/2 cup unsweetened almond milk
- 3 eggs
- 1/2 cup diced pineapple
- 1/2 cup diced mango
- 2 oz diced chicken breast or turkey breast (optional)

Directions:
1. In a medium bowl, whisk together the almond flour, coconut flour, baking powder, and salt.
2. In a separate small bowl, whisk together the almond milk and eggs.
3. Pour the wet ingredients into the dry ingredients and mix until just combined. Do not overmix.
4. Stir in the diced pineapple and mango.
5. Heat a non-stick pan or griddle over medium heat. Once hot, spoon 1/4 cup of the pancake batter onto the pan for each pancake.
6. Cook the pancakes for 1-2 minutes on each side, or until golden brown.
7. Serve the pancakes hot with diced chicken breast or turkey breast (if using) as a lean protein option. Enjoy!

Nutrition (per serving): Calories: 170, Fat: 14g, Carbohydrates: 6g, Protein: 8g, Sodium: 260mg

Chocolate Cake with Peanut Butter Filling

Prep Time: 20 minutes **Cook time:** 35 minutes **Serving:** 8

Ingredients:
- 1 cup almond flour
- 1/4 cup unsweetened cocoa powder
- 1 tsp baking powder
- 1/2 tsp salt
- 1/2 cup unsweetened almond milk
- 1/4 cup sugar-free maple syrup
- 2 egg whites
- 1 tsp vanilla extract
- 1/4 cup natural peanut butter

Directions:
1. Preheat the oven to 350°F (180°C). Grease and flour a 9-inch round cake pan.
2. In a large bowl, whisk together the almond flour, cocoa powder, baking powder, and salt.
3. In a separate small bowl, whisk together the almond milk, maple syrup, egg whites, and vanilla extract.
4. Pour the wet ingredients into the dry ingredients and mix until just combined. Do not overmix.
5. Pour the batter into the prepared cake pan.
6. Bake the cake for 30-35 minutes, or until a toothpick inserted into the center comes out clean.
7. Allow the cake to cool in the pan for 10 minutes, then transfer it to a wire rack to cool completely.
8. Once the cake is cooled, spread the natural peanut butter over the top of the cake.
9. Serve the cake and enjoy!

Nutrition (per serving): Calories: 200, Fat: 13g, Carbohydrates: 11g, Protein: 7g, Sodium: 190mg

Chocolate Chip Cakes

Prep Time: 15 minutes **Cook time:** 25 minutes **Serving:** 12

Ingredients:

- 1 1/2 cups all-purpose flour
- 1 tsp baking powder
- 1/2 tsp salt
- 1/2 cup unsalted butter, softened
- 3/4 cup granulated sugar
- 2 large eggs
- 1 tsp vanilla extract
- 1/2 cup milk
- 1 cup semisweet chocolate chips

Directions:

1. Preheat the oven to 350°F (180°C). Grease and flour a 12-cup muffin tin.
2. In a medium bowl, whisk together the flour, baking powder, and salt.
3. In a separate large bowl, beat the butter and sugar together until light and fluffy.
4. Beat in the eggs one at a time, then stir in the vanilla extract.
5. Add the dry ingredients to the butter mixture in three parts, alternating with the milk and starting and ending with the dry ingredients. Mix until just combined.
6. Stir in the chocolate chips.
7. Divide the batter evenly among the muffin cups.
8. Bake the cakes for 20-25 minutes, or until a toothpick inserted into the center comes out clean.
9. Allow the cakes to cool in the tin for 5 minutes, then transfer them to a wire rack to cool completely.
10. Serve the cakes and enjoy!

Nutrition (per serving): Calories: 170, Fat: 7g, Carbohydrates: 22g, Protein: 7g, Sodium: 220mg.

Breakfast Scramble

Prep Time: 10 minutes **Cook time:** 10 minutes **Serving:** 1

Ingredients:

- 1 cup of spinach, washed and chopped
- 1/2 cup of diced bell pepper (red, yellow or green)
- 1/2 cup of diced onion
- 1/2 cup of diced mushrooms
- 1/4 cup of diced tomatoes
- 4 eggs
- Salt and pepper, to taste

Directions:

1. Heat a skillet over medium heat and add a tablespoon of olive oil.
2. Add the diced bell pepper, onion, and mushrooms to the skillet and sauté for 2-3 minutes until they start to soften.
3. Add the chopped spinach and tomatoes to the skillet and continue to sauté for another 2-3 minutes.
4. Crack the eggs into the skillet and stir everything together.
5. Season with salt and pepper to taste.
6. Cook for 2-3 minutes, or until the eggs are fully cooked.

7. Serve the breakfast scramble in a bowl and enjoy!

Nutrition (per serving): Calories: 234, Protein: 17.5g, Fat: 15.6g, Carbohydrates: 8.2g, Fiber: 3.2g, Sugar: 4.1g

Breakfast Smoothie

Prep Time: 5 minutes **Serving:** 1

Ingredients:
- 1 cup of spinach, washed
- 1/2 cup of diced cucumber
- 1 small banana
- 1/2 cup of almond milk
- 1/4 cup of Greek yogurt
- 1/2 teaspoon of honey (optional)

Directions:
1. Add all ingredients to a blender and blend until smooth.
2. Taste and add more honey if needed.
3. Pour into a glass and enjoy!

Nutrition (per serving): Calories: 208, Protein: 12g, Fat: 6.5g, Carbohydrates: 29g, Fiber: 4.1g, Sugar: 13g

Breakfast Wrap

Prep Time: 5 minutes **Serving:** 1

Ingredients:
- 2 whole wheat tortillas
- 2 tablespoons of hummus
- 1/4 cup of diced bell pepper (red, yellow or green)
- 1/4 cup of diced onion
- 1/4 cup of diced mushrooms
- 1/4 cup of diced tomatoes
- 1/4 cup of feta cheese
- Salt and pepper, to taste
- 2 eggs

Directions:
1. In a skillet, heat a tablespoon of olive oil over medium heat.
2. Add the diced bell pepper, onion, and mushrooms to the skillet and sauté for 2-3 minutes until they start to soften.
3. Add the diced tomatoes, salt, and pepper and continue to sauté for another 2-3 minutes.
4. Crack the eggs into the skillet, stir until cook and set aside.
5. Spread hummus on one side of each tortilla.
6. Add the sautéed vegetables, feta cheese, and eggs on top of the hummus.
7. Roll up the tortilla and cut in half.
8. Serve and enjoy!

Nutrition (per serving): Calories: 348, Protein: 18g, Fat: 16g, Carbohydrates: 34g, Fiber: 5g Sugar: 5g

Chapter 2: Meat Recipes

Crispy Pork Cutlets

Prep Time: 15 minutes **Cook time:** 10 minutes **Serving:** 4

Ingredients:

- 4 boneless pork loin chops, about 1/4 inch thick
- Salt and pepper, to taste
- 1 cup almond flour
- 2 large egg whites, beaten
- 1 cup panko breadcrumbs
- 1 tbsp olive oil

Directions:

1. Season the pork chops with salt and pepper.
2. Place the almond flour, egg whites, and panko breadcrumbs in separate shallow bowls. Dip the pork chops first in the almond flour, then in the egg whites, and then in the panko breadcrumbs, making sure to coat each chop evenly.
3. Heat the olive oil in a large skillet over medium-high heat.
4. Once the oil is hot, add the pork chops to the skillet and cook for 2-3 minutes on each side, or until they are crispy and golden brown.
5. Transfer the pork chops to a plate lined with paper towels to drain any excess oil.
6. Serve the pork chops hot and enjoy!

Nutrition (per serving): Calories: 280, Fat: 9g, Carbohydrates: 12g, Protein: 32g, Sodium: 480mg

Herb Ground Beef

Prep Time: 15 minutes **Cook time:** 10 minutes **Serving:** 4

Ingredients:

- 1 lb lean ground beef (90/10)
- 1 small onion, finely chopped
- 1 small carrot, finely chopped
- 2 cloves garlic, minced
- 1 tsp dried basil
- 1 tsp dried oregano
- 1 tsp dried thyme
- Salt and pepper, to taste
- 1 tbsp olive oil

Directions:

1. In a large skillet, heat the olive oil over medium-high heat.
2. Add the ground beef, onion, carrot, and garlic to the skillet and cook until the beef is browned and the vegetables are tender, about 5-7 minutes.
3. Stir in the basil, oregano, and thyme, and season with salt and pepper.
4. Serve the ground beef hot and enjoy!

Nutrition (per serving): Calories: 220, Fat: 12g, Carbohydrates: 5g, Protein: 26g, Sodium: 90mg

Roasted Sirloin Steak

Prep Time: 5 minutes **Cook time:** 15 minutes **Serving:** 4

Ingredients:
- 1 lb sirloin steak
- 1 tbsp olive oil
- Salt and pepper, to taste

Directions:
1. Preheat your oven to 450°F.
2. Brush the sirloin steak with olive oil and season with salt and pepper.
3. Place the steak in a baking dish and roast in the preheated oven for 10-15 minutes, or until the steak reaches your desired level of doneness.
4. Let the steak rest for 5 minutes before slicing and serving.

Nutrition (per serving): Calories: 280, Fat: 17g, Carbohydrates: 0g, Protein: 30g, Sodium: 85mg

Baked Turkey Patties

Prep Time: 15 minutes **Cook time:** 20 minutes **Serving:** 4

Ingredients:
- 1 pound ground turkey
- 1/2 cup rolled oats
- 1 egg white
- 1/4 cup diced onion
- 1/4 cup diced bell pepper
- 1 tsp dried thyme
- 1 tsp dried oregano
- Salt and pepper, to taste
- 1 tbsp olive oil

Directions:
1. Preheat your oven to 400 degrees F (200 degrees C). Line a baking sheet with parchment paper.
2. In a large mixing bowl, combine the ground turkey, rolled oats, egg white, diced onion, diced bell pepper, thyme, oregano, salt, and pepper. Mix until well combined.
3. Divide the mixture into 4 equal parts and shape into patties. Place the patties onto the prepared baking sheet.
4. Brush the patties with olive oil.
5. Bake the patties in the preheated oven for 20 minutes, or until they are cooked through and the internal temperature reaches 165 degrees F (74 degrees C).
6. Serve the patties with a serving of vegetables as a green option and enjoy!

Nutrition (per serving): Calories: 198, Fat: 10g, Carbohydrates: 10g, Protein: 21g, Sodium: 132mg

Beef Patties

Prep Time: 20 minutes **Cook time:** 10 minutes **Serving:** 4

Ingredients:
- 1 pound ground beef

- 1 small onion, finely chopped
- 1 clove garlic, minced
- 1 egg
- 1/4 cup breadcrumbs
- 1 tablespoon Worcestershire sauce
- 1/2 teaspoon salt
- 1/4 teaspoon pepper
- 1 tablespoon oil

Directions:
1. In a large bowl, mix together the ground beef, onion, garlic, egg, breadcrumbs, Worcestershire sauce, salt, and pepper.
2. Shape the mixture into 4 patties.
3. Heat the oil in a large skillet over medium heat. Add the patties and cook for about 5 minutes on each side, or until they are cooked to your desired level of doneness.
4. Serve the patties on hamburger buns or with your choice of sides. Enjoy!

Nutrition (per serving): Fat: 18g, Net Carbs: 8g, Protein: 22g, Sodium: 360mg

Feta Lamb Patties

Prep Time: 20 minutes **Cook time:** 10 minutes **Serving:** 4

Ingredients:
- 1 pound ground lamb
- 1/4 cup crumbled feta cheese
- 1/4 cup chopped fresh mint
- 1 clove garlic, minced
- 1 egg
- 1/4 cup breadcrumbs
- 1 teaspoon cumin
- 1/2 teaspoon salt
- 1/4 teaspoon pepper
- 1 tablespoon olive oil

Directions:
1. In a large bowl, mix together the ground lamb, feta cheese, mint, garlic, egg, breadcrumbs, cumin, salt, and pepper.
2. Shape the mixture into 4 patties.
3. Heat the oil in a large skillet over medium heat. Add the patties and cook for about 5 minutes on each side, or until they are cooked to your desired level of doneness.
4. Serve the patties on hamburger buns or with your choice of sides. Enjoy!

Nutrition (per serving): Fat: 14g, Net Carbs: 6g, Protein: 27g, Sodium: 460mg

Grilled Chicken Stroganoff

Prep Time: 20 minutes **Cook time:** 15 minutes **Serving:** 4

Ingredients:
- 4 boneless, skinless chicken breasts, thinly sliced
- 1 medium onion, thinly sliced
- 2 cloves garlic, minced
- 8 ounces sliced mushrooms
- 1 cup chicken broth
- 1/2 cup sour cream
- 2 tablespoons all-purpose flour
- 1 tablespoon olive oil
- 1/2 teaspoon salt
- 1/4 teaspoon black pepper
- 1/4 cup chopped fresh parsley
- 4 cups cooked whole wheat pasta

Directions:
1. In a large skillet, heat the oil over medium-high heat. Add the chicken and cook for about 2-3 minutes, or until it is browned on all sides.
2. Add the onion, garlic, and mushrooms to the skillet. Cook for an additional 2-3 minutes, or until the vegetables are tender.
3. Stir in the chicken broth and flour. Bring the mixture to a boil, then reduce the heat to a simmer.
4. Simmer for about 10 minutes, or until the sauce has thickened.
5. Stir in the sour cream, salt, and pepper. Cook for an additional 2-3 minutes, or until the sauce is heated through.
6. Stir in the parsley. Serve the chicken stroganoff over the cooked whole wheat pasta. Enjoy!

Nutrition (per serving): Fat: 15g, Net Carbs: 21g, Protein: 33g, Sodium: 590mg (based on using whole wheat pasta)

Beef Ribeye Steak

Prep Time: 5 minutes **Cook time:** 10-15 minutes **Serving:** 4

Ingredients:
- 4 beef ribeye steaks about 1 inch thick
- 1 tablespoon olive oil
- 1 teaspoon salt
- 1/2 teaspoon black pepper

Directions:
1. Preheat your grill or broiler to high heat.
2. Rub the steaks with oil and season them with salt and pepper on both sides.
3. Place the steaks on the grill or under the broiler. Grill for about 5-7 minutes on each side for medium-rare, or longer if you prefer your steaks more well-done.
4. Let the steaks rest for about 5 minutes before slicing and serving. Enjoy!

Nutrition (per serving): Calories: 210, Fat: 9g, Carbohydrates: 0g, Protein: 28g, Sodium: 340mg

Roast Beef

Prep Time: 15 minutes **Cook time:** 2-3 hours **Serving:** 4-6

Ingredients:

- 2-3 pound beef roast (such as sirloin or rump roast)
- 1 tablespoon olive oil
- 1 teaspoon salt
- 1/2 teaspoon black pepper
- 1/2 cup beef broth
- 2 cloves garlic, minced
- 1 medium onion, quartered
- 1 large carrot, chopped
- 1 stalk celery, chopped

Directions:

1. Preheat your oven to 300°F (150°C).
2. In a large oven-safe pot or Dutch oven, heat the oil over medium-high heat. Season the roast with salt and pepper on all sides.
3. Place the roast in the pot and sear it on all sides until it is browned, about 2-3 minutes per side.
4. Add the beef broth, garlic, onion, carrot, and celery to the pot. Cover the pot and place it in the preheated oven.
5. Roast the beef for 2-3 hours, or until it is tender and reaches an internal temperature of 145°F (63°C) for medium-rare.
6. Remove the pot from the oven and let the roast rest for about 10-15 minutes before slicing and serving. Enjoy!

Nutrition (per serving): Fat: 6g, Net Carbs: 3g, Protein: 40g, Sodium: 480mg

Beef Korma

Prep Time: 20 minutes **Cook time:** 30 minutes **Serving:** 4

Ingredients:

- 1 lb lean beef sirloin or flank steak, cut into 1-inch cubes
- 1 tbsp olive oil
- 1 small onion, finely chopped
- 2 cloves garlic, minced
- 1 tbsp grated ginger
- 1 tsp ground coriander
- 1 tsp ground cumin
- 1/2 tsp ground turmeric
- 1/2 tsp ground cardamom
- 1/2 tsp ground cinnamon
- 1/2 cup low-sodium beef broth
- 1/4 cup plain Greek yogurt
- Salt and pepper to taste
- 1/4 cup chopped fresh cilantro

Directions:
1. In a large skillet, heat the olive oil over medium-high heat. Add the beef and cook until it is browned on all sides, about 5-7 minutes.
2. Add the onion, garlic, and ginger to the skillet. Cook for an additional 2-3 minutes, or until the vegetables are tender.
3. Stir in the coriander, cumin, turmeric, cardamom, and cinnamon. Cook for an additional 1-2 minutes, or until the spices are fragrant.
4. Stir in the beef broth and Greek yogurt. Bring the mixture to a boil, then reduce the heat to a simmer.
5. Season with salt and pepper to taste.
6. Simmer for about 20-25 minutes, or until the beef is tender.
7. Stir in the cilantro.
8. Serve the beef korma over cauliflower rice or a side of vegetables of your choice. Enjoy!

Nutrition (per serving): Calories: 250, Fat: 11g, Carbohydrates: 7g, Protein: 32g, Sodium: 260mg

Sheet Pan Chicken Fajita Lettuce Wraps

Prep Time: 15 minutes **Cook time:** 20 minutes **Serving:** 4

Ingredients:
- 1 pound boneless, skinless chicken breasts, cut into thin strips
- 1 red bell pepper, thinly sliced
- 1 green bell pepper, thinly sliced
- 1 yellow bell pepper, thinly sliced
- 1 medium onion, thinly sliced
- 1 tablespoon oil
- 1 teaspoon chili powder
- 1/2 teaspoon ground cumin
- 1/2 teaspoon paprika
- 1/2 teaspoon salt
- 8 large lettuce leaves
- 1/2 cup salsa
- 1/2 cup shredded cheese

Directions:
1. Preheat your oven to 425°F (220°C).
2. In a large bowl, mix together the chicken, bell peppers, onion, oil, chili powder, cumin, paprika, and salt.
3. Transfer the mixture to a large sheet pan and spread it out evenly.
4. Bake the chicken and vegetables for about 20 minutes, or until the chicken is cooked through and the vegetables are tender.
5. To assemble the lettuce wraps, spoon some of the chicken and vegetables mixture onto the center of each lettuce leaf. Top with salsa and shredded cheese.
6. Roll up the lettuce leaves and enjoy!

Nutrition (per serving): Fat: 17g, Net Carbs: 11g, Protein: 27g, Sodium: 480mg

Lemon Garlic Oregano Chicken with Asparagus

Prep Time: 10 minutes **Cook time:** 20 minutes **Serving:** 4

Ingredients:
- 4 boneless, skinless chicken breasts
- 1 tablespoon olive oil
- 4 cloves garlic, minced
- 1 teaspoon dried oregano
- 1/2 teaspoon salt
- 1/4 teaspoon black pepper
- 1 pound asparagus, trimmed
- 1 lemon, thinly sliced

Directions:
1. Preheat your oven to 400°F (200°C).
2. In a small bowl, mix together the olive oil, garlic, oregano, salt, and pepper.
3. Place the chicken breasts in a large baking dish and brush them with the olive oil mixture.
4. Arrange the asparagus and lemon slices around the chicken.
5. Bake the chicken and vegetables for about 20 minutes, or until the chicken is cooked through and the asparagus is tender.
6. Serve the chicken and vegetables with your choice of side dishes. Enjoy!

Nutrition (per serving): Fat: 8g, Net Carbs: 6g, Protein: 30g, Sodium: 420mg

Chipotle Chicken and Cauliflower Rice Bowls

Prep Time: 10 minutes **Cook time:** 20 minutes **Serving:** 4

Ingredients:
- 4 boneless, skinless chicken breasts
- 1 tablespoon olive oil
- 2 cloves garlic, minced
- 1 teaspoon ground cumin
- 1 teaspoon chili powder
- 1/2 teaspoon salt
- 1/4 teaspoon black pepper
- 1 cup uncooked cauliflower rice
- 1/4 cup chipotle sauce
- 1 cup black beans, drained and rinsed
- 1/4 cup chopped cilantro

Directions:
1. Preheat your oven to 400°F (200°C).
2. In a small bowl, mix together the olive oil, garlic, cumin, chili powder, salt, and pepper.
3. Place the chicken breasts in a large baking dish and brush them with the olive oil mixture.
4. Bake the chicken for about 20 minutes, or until it is cooked through.
5. Meanwhile, cook the cauliflower rice according to the package instructions.

6. Slice the chicken and mix it together with the cauliflower rice, chipotle sauce, black beans, and cilantro in a large bowl.
7. Serve the chicken and cauliflower rice mixture in bowls. Enjoy!

Nutrition: Fat: 12g, Net Carbs: 8g, Protein: 31g, Sodium: 380mg

Chicken Caesar Salad

Prep Time: 10 minutes **Cook time:** 20 minutes **Serving:** 4

Ingredients:
- 4 boneless, skinless chicken breasts
- 1 tablespoon olive oil
- 1 teaspoon dried oregano
- 1/2 teaspoon salt
- 1/4 teaspoon black pepper
- 1/4 cup low-fat Caesar salad dressing
- 1 head romaine lettuce, chopped
- 1/2 cup croutons
- 1/4 cup grated Parmesan cheese

Directions:
1. Preheat your grill to medium-high heat.
2. In a small bowl, mix together the olive oil, oregano, salt, and pepper.
3. Brush the chicken breasts with the olive oil mixture.
4. Grill the chicken for about 5-7 minutes on each side, or until it is cooked through.
5. Meanwhile, mix together the Caesar salad dressing, lettuce, croutons, and Parmesan cheese in a large bowl.
6. Slice the chicken and add it to the salad. Toss the salad to combine all of the ingredients.
7. Serve the salad immediately. Enjoy!

Nutrition (per serving): Fat: 12g, Net Carbs: 6g, Protein: 29g, Sodium: 480mg

Mediterranean Chicken and Vegetables

Prep Time: 20 minutes **Cook time:** 20 minutes **Serving:** 4

Ingredients:
- 4 chicken breasts
- 1 head of broccoli, chopped
- 1 head of cauliflower, chopped
- 1 red onion, sliced
- 1/4 cup olive oil
- 2 cloves garlic, minced
- 1 tsp dried oregano
- 1 tsp dried basil
- 1/2 tsp dried thyme

- 1/2 tsp salt
- 1/4 tsp black pepper
- 1/4 cup feta cheese

Directions
1. Preheat your oven to 400°F.
2. Line a baking sheet with parchment paper.
3. In a small bowl, mix together the olive oil, garlic, oregano, basil, thyme, salt, and pepper.
4. Place the chicken breasts on the prepared baking sheet. Brush the olive oil mixture over the chicken breasts. Arrange the chopped broccoli, cauliflower, and onion around the chicken.
5. Bake for 20 minutes, or until the chicken is cooked through and the vegetables are tender.
6. Sprinkle feta cheese over the top of the chicken and vegetables.
7. Serve immediately.

Nutrition (per serving): Fat: 18g, Net Carbs: 7g, Protein: 36g, Sodium: 390mg

Shredded Beef Stew

Prep Time: 10 minutes **Cook time:** 2 hours **Serving:** 4

Ingredients:
- 1 lb lean beef sirloin or top round, trimmed of excess fat
- 1 tablespoon canola oil
- 1 medium onion, chopped
- 2 cloves garlic, minced
- 2 cups low-sodium beef broth
- 1 cup water
- 1 tablespoon tomato paste
- 1 teaspoon dried oregano
- 1 teaspoon dried basil
- 1/2 teaspoon salt
- 1/4 teaspoon black pepper
- 2 medium carrots, peeled and cut into
- 1/4-inch slices
- 1 medium parsnip, peeled and cut into
- 1/4-inch slices
- 1 medium rutabaga, peeled and cut into
- 1/4-inch slices
- 1/2 cup frozen peas

Directions:
1. Preheat your oven to 300°F.
2. Cut the beef into 1-inch cubes and set aside.
3. Heat the canola oil in a large, heavy-bottomed pot over medium heat. Add the onion and garlic and cook until the onion is translucent, about 5 minutes.
4. Add the beef cubes to the pot and cook until they are browned on all sides.
5. Add the low-sodium beef broth, water, tomato paste, oregano, basil, salt, and pepper to the pot. Bring the mixture to a boil, then reduce the heat to low.

6. Cover the pot and transfer it to the preheated oven. Cook for 1 1/2 hours.
7. After 1 1/2 hours, add the carrots, parsnip, and rutabaga to the pot. Cover and return to the oven for an additional 30 minutes.
8. After the stew has cooked for a total of 2 hours, remove the pot from the oven. Stir in the frozen peas.
9. Serve the stew hot, garnished with additional chopped herbs if desired.

Nutrition (per serving): Fat: 6g, Net Carbs: 18g, Protein: 27g, Sodium: 480mg

Grilled Chicken and Vegetable Paella

Prep Time: 15 minutes **Cook time**: 20 minutes **Serving**: 4

Ingredients:
- 4 boneless, skinless chicken breasts
- 1 tablespoon olive oil
- 1 teaspoon smoked paprika
- 1/2 teaspoon salt
- 1/4 teaspoon black pepper
- 1 medium onion, diced
- 1 red bell pepper, diced
- 1 green bell pepper, diced
- 2 cloves garlic, minced
- 1 head of cauliflower, grated
- 2 cups chicken broth
- 1/2 cup white wine
- 1 teaspoon paprika
- 1/2 teaspoon saffron
- 1/4 teaspoon cumin
- 1/4 teaspoon oregano
- 1/4 teaspoon thyme
- 1 cup frozen peas

Directions:
1. Preheat a grill or grill pan to medium-high heat.
2. In a small bowl, mix together the olive oil, smoked paprika, salt, and pepper.
3. Place the chicken breasts in the bowl and toss to coat with the marinade.
4. Grill the chicken for 6-8 minutes per side or until cooked through. Remove from grill and let it cool. Once cooled, shred the chicken.
5. In a large pot or Dutch oven, heat some olive oil over medium heat. Add the onion, bell peppers, and garlic and cook until the vegetables are tender.
6. Stir in the grated cauliflower and cook for 1-2 minutes until the cauliflower is lightly toasted.
7. Add the chicken broth, white wine, paprika, saffron, cumin, oregano, thyme, salt, and pepper to the pot and bring to a boil.
8. Reduce the heat to low, and add the shredded chicken and frozen peas.
9. Cover the pot and simmer for about 20 minutes or until the cauliflower is cooked through and the liquid has been absorbed.

10. Serve hot and enjoy!

Nutrition (per serving): Fat: 8g, Net Carbs: 10g, Protein: 34g, Sodium: 360mg

Chicken Meatballs and Napa Cabbage in Ginger Broth

Prep Time: 15 minutes **Cook time:** 45 minutes **Serving:** 4

Ingredients:

For the meatballs:

- 1 pound ground chicken
- 1/4 cup almond flour
- 1 egg
- 1/4 cup finely chopped green onions
- 1 clove garlic, minced
- 1 teaspoon coconut aminos
- 1 teaspoon sesame oil

For the broth:

- 6 cups chicken broth
- 1 (2-inch) piece ginger, sliced
- 1/4 cup coconut aminos
- 1 tablespoon fish sauce
- 1/4 cup rice wine vinegar
- 1/4 cup Swerve or other sugar substitute
- 1/4 teaspoon black pepper
- 1/2 head napa cabbage, chopped

Directions:

1. In a large mixing bowl, combine the ground chicken, almond flour, egg, green onions, garlic, coconut aminos, and sesame oil. Mix well until all the ingredients are evenly distributed.
2. Shape the mixture into small meatballs, about 1 inch in diameter.
3. In a large pot, bring the chicken broth, ginger, coconut aminos, fish sauce, rice wine vinegar, Swerve, and black pepper to a boil.
4. Add the meatballs to the pot and simmer for 15 minutes or until they are cooked through.
5. Add the napa cabbage to the pot and cook for an additional 5 minutes or until it is tender.
6. Serve the meatballs and cabbage in bowls with the broth. Enjoy!

Nutrition (per serving): Fat: 11g, Net Carbs: 3g, Protein: 29g, Sodium: 815mg

Parmesan Meatballs with Collard Greens

Prep Time: 15 minutes **Cook time:** 25 minutes **Serving:** 4

Ingredients:

For the meatballs:

- 1 pound lean ground turkey
- 1/4 cup grated Parmesan cheese
- 1 egg white
- 1/4 cup whole wheat breadcrumbs

- 1 clove garlic, minced
- 1 teaspoon Italian seasoning
- 1/4 teaspoon salt
- 1/4 teaspoon black pepper

For the collard greens:
- 1 tablespoon olive oil
- 1 medium onion, diced
- 3 cloves garlic, minced
- 1 bunch collard greens, stems removed and leaves chopped
- 1/4 cup chicken broth
- 1/4 teaspoon salt
- 1/4 teaspoon black pepper

Directions:
1. Preheat your oven to 400°F (200°C). Line a baking sheet with parchment paper.
2. In a large mixing bowl, combine the ground turkey, Parmesan cheese, egg white, whole wheat breadcrumbs, garlic, Italian seasoning, salt, and pepper. Mix well until all the ingredients are evenly distributed.
3. Shape the mixture into small meatballs, about 1 inch in diameter. Place the meatballs on the prepared baking sheet.
4. Bake the meatballs for 15-20 minutes or until they are cooked through.
5. While the meatballs are cooking, heat the olive oil in a large pan over medium heat. Add the onion and garlic and cook until the onion is translucent.
6. Add the collard greens, chicken broth, salt, and pepper to the pan and cook for 5-7 minutes or until the collard greens are tender.
7. Serve the meatballs and collard greens hot and enjoy!

Nutrition (per serving): Fat: 8g, Net Carbs: 7g, Protein: 38g, Sodium: 383mg

Lean and Green Grilled Chicken

Prep Time: 10 minutes + marinade time **Cook time:** 20 minutes **Serving:** 4

Ingredients:
- 4 boneless, skinless chicken breasts
- 2 tablespoons of olive oil
- 2 cloves of minced garlic
- 1 teaspoon of dried thyme
- 1/2 teaspoon of dried rosemary
- Salt and pepper, to taste
- 1 cup of mixed green vegetables (such as broccoli, asparagus, and green beans)

Directions:
1. In a small bowl, mix together olive oil, minced garlic, thyme, rosemary, salt, and pepper.
2. Place the chicken breasts in a shallow dish and pour the marinade over them. Make sure the chicken is well coated.
3. Cover and refrigerate for at least 30 minutes, or up to 2 hours.
4. Preheat the grill to medium-high heat.
5. Grill the chicken for 4-5 minutes per side, or until the internal temperature reaches 165°F.

6. In a separate skillet, heat a tablespoon of olive oil over medium heat.
7. Add the mixed green vegetables, salt and pepper and sauté for 2-3 minutes until they start to soften.
8. Serve the grilled chicken with the sautéed mixed green vegetables and enjoy!

Nutrition (per serving): Calories: 225, Protein: 29g, Fat: 10g, Carbohydrates: 3g, Fiber: 1g, Sugar: 1g

Turkey and Vegetable Stir-Fry

Prep Time: 10 minutes **Cook time:** 15 minutes **Serving:** 4

Ingredients:
- 1 pound of turkey breast, sliced thin
- 2 tablespoons of olive oil
- 2 cloves of minced garlic
- 1/2 cup of diced bell pepper (red, yellow or green)
- 1/2 cup of diced onion
- 1/2 cup of diced mushrooms
- 1/2 cup of diced zucchini
- 1/4 cup of low-sodium soy sauce
- 1 teaspoon of cornstarch
- 1/4 cup of chicken broth
- Salt and pepper, to taste
- 1 cup of chopped kale

Directions:
1. In a small bowl, mix together soy sauce, cornstarch, and chicken broth. Set aside.
2. In a large skillet or wok, heat 1 tablespoon of olive oil over high heat.
3. Add the turkey and stir-fry for 3-4 minutes, or until cooked through. Remove from skillet and set aside.
4. In the same skillet, heat the remaining olive oil over high heat.
5. Add the garlic, bell pepper, onion, mushrooms, and zucchini. Stir-fry for 2-3 minutes, or until vegetables are tender.
6. Add the soy sauce mixture, salt and pepper, and stir-fry for 1-2 minutes, or until the sauce thickens.
7. Add the turkey back in the skillet and stir-fry for another minute.
8. Add the chopped kale and stir-fry for another minute or until the kale is wilted.
9. Serve and enjoy!

Nutrition (per serving): Calories: 216, Protein: 29g, Fat: 8g, Carbohydrates: 7g, Fiber: 2g, Sugar: 3g

Chapter 3: Fish and Seafood Recipes

Scallops and Sweet Potatoes

Prep Time: 10 minutes **Cook time:** 20 minutes **Serving:** 4

Ingredients:
- 1 pound scallops
- 1 sweet potato, peeled and diced
- 1 tablespoon olive oil
- 1/4 teaspoon salt-free seasoning blend (e.g. Mrs. Dash)

Directions:
1. Preheat your oven to 400°F (200°C).
2. Place the diced sweet potato on a baking sheet and toss with the olive oil and seasoning blend. Spread the sweet potatoes in an even layer.
3. Roast the sweet potatoes for 15-20 minutes or until they are tender.
4. While the sweet potatoes are cooking, heat a large pan over medium-high heat. Add the scallops and cook for 2-3 minutes on each side or until they are browned and cooked through.
5. Serve the scallops and sweet potatoes hot and enjoy!

Nutrition (per serving): Fat: 5g, Net Carbs: 15g, Protein: 20g, Sodium: 103mg

Salmon and Shrimp Salad

Prep Time: 10 minutes **Cook time:** 15 minutes **Serving:** 4

Ingredients:

For the salmon and shrimp:
- 1 pound skinless salmon, cut into 4 pieces
- 1 pound large shrimp, peeled and deveined
- 1 tablespoon olive oil
- 1/4 teaspoon salt-free seasoning blend (e.g. Mrs. Dash)

For the salad:
- 4 cups mixed greens
- 1/2 cup cherry tomatoes, halved
- 1/4 cup sliced cucumber
- 1/4 cup crumbled low-fat feta cheese
- 1/4 cup chopped red onion
- 1/4 cup sliced olives
- 1/4 cup sliced bell peppers
- 1/4 cup cooked quinoa (optional)

For the dressing:
- 1 tablespoons balsamic vinegar

- 1 tablespoon Dijon mustard
- 1 clove garlic, minced
- 1/4 teaspoon dried basil
- 1/4 teaspoon dried oregano
- pepper to taste

Directions:
1. Preheat your oven to 400°F (200°C). Line a baking sheet with parchment paper.
2. Place the salmon and shrimp on the prepared baking sheet and brush with the olive oil. Sprinkle with the salt-free seasoning blend.
3. Roast the salmon and shrimp for 10-15 minutes or until they are cooked through.
4. While the salmon and shrimp are cooking, prepare the salad by placing the mixed greens, cherry tomatoes, cucumber, feta cheese, red onion, olives, bell peppers, and quinoa (if using) in a large mixing bowl.
5. In a small mixing bowl, whisk together the balsamic vinegar, Dijon mustard, garlic, dried basil, dried oregano, pepper to make the dressing.
6. When the salmon and shrimp are cooked, add them to the salad and drizzle with the dressing. Toss to combine.
7. Serve the salad hot and enjoy!

Nutrition (per serving): Fat: 12g, Net Carbs: 8g, Protein: 34g, Sodium: 420mg

Shrimp, Tomato and Dates Salad

Prep Time: 15 minutes **Cook time:** 5 minutes **Serving:** 4

Ingredients:
- 1 pound large shrimp, peeled and deveined
- 1 tablespoon olive oil
- 1/4 teaspoon salt-free seasoning blend (e.g. Mrs. Dash)
- 4 cups mixed greens
- 1 cup cherry tomatoes, halved
- 1/4 cup chopped red onion
- 1/4 cup crumbled low-fat feta cheese

For the dressing:
- 2 tablespoons balsamic vinegar
- 1 tablespoon Dijon mustard
- 1 clove garlic, minced
- 1/4 teaspoon dried basil
- 1/4 teaspoon dried oregano
- pepper to taste
- 1 tablespoons extra virgin olive oil

Directions:
1. Heat a large pan over medium-high heat. Add the shrimp and cook for 2-3 minutes on each side or until they are pink and cooked through. Remove the shrimp from the pan and set aside.

2. In a large mixing bowl, combine the mixed greens, cherry tomatoes, red onion, and feta cheese.
3. In a small mixing bowl, whisk together the balsamic vinegar, Dijon mustard, garlic, dried basil, dried oregano, pepper and olive oil to make the dressing.
4. Add the cooked shrimp to the salad and drizzle with the dressing. Toss to combine.
5. Serve the salad hot and enjoy!

Nutrition (per serving): Fat: 14g, Net Carbs: 8g, Protein: 25g, Sodium: 380mg

Salmon and Watercress Salad

Prep Time: 10 minutes **Cook time:** 15 minutes **Serving:** 4

Ingredients:

For the salmon:
- 1 pound salmon, cut into 4 pieces
- 1 tablespoon olive oil
- 1/4 teaspoon salt-free seasoning blend (e.g. Mrs. Dash)

For the salad:
- 4 cups watercress
- 1/2 cup cherry tomatoes, halved
- 1/4 cup sliced cucumber
- 1/4 cup crumbled low-fat feta cheese
- 1/4 cup chopped red onion
- 1/4 cup sliced olives
- 1/4 cup sliced bell peppers
- 1/4 cup cooked quinoa (optional)

For the dressing:
- 2 tablespoons balsamic vinegar
- 1 tablespoon Dijon mustard
- 1 clove garlic, minced
- 1/4 teaspoon dried basil
- 1/4 teaspoon dried oregano
- pepper to taste
- 1 tablespoons extra virgin olive oil

Directions:
1. Preheat your oven to 400°F (200°C). Line a baking sheet with parchment paper.
2. Place the salmon on the prepared baking sheet and brush with the olive oil. Sprinkle with the salt-free seasoning blend.
3. Roast the salmon for 10-15 minutes or until it is cooked through.
4. While the salmon is cooking, prepare the salad by placing the watercress, cherry tomatoes, cucumber, feta cheese, red onion, olives, bell peppers, and quinoa (if using) in a large mixing bowl.

5. In a small mixing bowl, whisk together the balsamic vinegar, Dijon mustard, garlic, dried basil, dried oregano, pepper and olive oil to make the dressing.
6. When the salmon is cooked, add it to the salad and drizzle with the dressing. Toss to combine.
7. Serve the salad hot and enjoy!

Nutrition (per serving): Fat: 14g, Net Carbs: 11g, Protein: 32g, Sodium: 186mg (without quinoa)

Savory Salmon with Cilantro

Prep Time: 5 minutes **Cook time:** 10 minutes **Serving:** 4

Ingredients:
- 4 salmon fillets
- 1/4 teaspoon salt
- 1/4 teaspoon black pepper
- 1 tablespoon olive oil
- 1/4 cup chopped cilantro

Directions:
1. Preheat your oven to 400°F (200°C). Line a baking sheet with parchment paper.
2. Place the salmon fillets on the prepared baking sheet and sprinkle with the salt and pepper.
3. Roast the salmon for 8-10 minutes or until it is cooked through.
4. While the salmon is cooking, heat a small pan over medium heat. Add the olive oil and chopped cilantro to the pan and cook for 1-2 minutes or until the cilantro is fragrant.
5. When the salmon is cooked, top it with the cilantro mixture.
6. Serve the salmon hot and enjoy!

Nutrition (per serving): Fat: 15g, Net Carbs: 0g, Protein: 24g, Sodium: 245mg

Middle Eastern Salmon with Tomatoes and Cucumber

Prep Time: 10 minutes **Cook time:** 10 minutes **Serving:** 4

Ingredients:
- 4 salmon fillets
- 1/4 teaspoon salt-free seasoning blend (e.g. Mrs. Dash)
- 1 tablespoon olive oil
- 4 cups mixed greens
- 1 cup cherry tomatoes, halved
- 1/2 cup sliced cucumber 1/4 cup chopped parsley
- 1/4 cup chopped red onion
- 1/4 cup sliced black olives
- 2 tablespoons lemon juice
- 1 tablespoon balsamic vinegar
- 1/4 teaspoon ground cumin
- 1/4 teaspoon ground coriander
- 1/4 teaspoon ground ginger

Directions:
1. Preheat your oven to 400°F (200°C). Line a baking sheet with parchment paper.

2. Place the salmon fillets on the prepared baking sheet and sprinkle with the salt-free seasoning blend.
3. Roast the salmon for 8-10 minutes or until it is cooked through.
4. While the salmon is cooking, prepare the salad by combining mixed greens, cherry tomatoes, cucumber, parsley, red onion, black olives, lemon juice, balsamic vinegar, cumin, coriander, and ginger in a large mixing bowl.
5. When the salmon is cooked, add it to the salad and toss to combine.
6. Serve the salad hot and enjoy!

Nutrition (per serving): Fat: 8g, Net Carbs: 8g, Protein: 32g, Sodium: 208mg

Grilled Salmon with Spinach and Parmesan

Prep Time: 10 minutes **Cook time:** 10 minutes **Serving:** 4

Ingredients:
- 4 (5-7 oz) wild-caught salmon fillets
- Salt and pepper, to taste
- 1 tbsp olive oil
- 2 cups baby spinach
- 1/4 cup grated Parmesan cheese
- Lemon wedges, for serving (optional)

Directions:
1. Preheat grill or grill pan to medium-high heat.
2. Season the salmon fillets with salt and pepper and brush with olive oil.
3. Grill the salmon for 3-4 minutes per side, or until the fish is cooked through.
4. In a pan over medium heat, sauté spinach until wilted. Season with salt and pepper.
5. Once the spinach is wilted, remove from heat and stir in Parmesan cheese.
6. Serve the salmon on a bed of spinach and Parmesan mixture, and lemon wedges on the side if desired.

Nutrition (per serving): Fat: 18g, Net Carbs: 2g, Protein: 25g, Sodium: 239mg

Grilled Tilapia with Lemon Herb Marinade

Prep Time: 10 minutes **Cook time:** 10 minutes **Serving:** 4

Ingredients:
- 4 tilapia fillets
- 1/4 teaspoon salt
- 1/4 teaspoon black pepper
- 1 tablespoon olive oil
- 1/4 cup lemon juice
- 1 tablespoon chopped fresh parsley
- 1 tablespoon chopped fresh cilantro
- 1 tablespoon chopped fresh basil
- 1 teaspoon minced garlic

Directions:

1. Mix the olive oil, lemon juice, parsley, cilantro, basil, and garlic in a small bowl.
2. Place the tilapia fillets in a shallow dish and season with salt and pepper.
3. Pour the marinade over the tilapia and let it marinate for at least 30 minutes in the refrigerator.
4. Preheat the grill to medium-high heat.
5. Remove the tilapia from the marinade and discard the remaining marinade.
6. Grill the tilapia for 4-5 minutes on each side or until it is cooked through.
7. Serve the tilapia hot and enjoy!

Nutrition (per serving): Fat: 5g, Net Carbs: 2g, Protein: 26g, Sodium: 474mg

Thai Curry Shrimp

Prep Time: 15 minutes **Cook time:** 20 minutes **Serving:** 4

Ingredients:
- 1 pound large shrimp, peeled and deveined
- 1 tablespoon vegetable oil
- 1 tablespoon red curry paste
- 1 cup light coconut milk
- 1 cup chicken broth
- 1 tablespoon brown sugar
- 1 tablespoon fish sauce
- 1/4 teaspoon salt
- 1/4 cup chopped fresh cilantro
- 2 cups steamed broccoli florets

Directions:
1. Heat the oil in a large saucepan over medium heat. Add the curry paste and cook, stirring, until fragrant, about 1 minute.
2. Add the coconut milk, chicken broth, brown sugar, fish sauce, and salt to the pan and bring to a boil. Reduce the heat to low and simmer for 5 minutes.
3. Add the shrimp to the pan and simmer until they are pink and cooked through, about 5 minutes.
4. Stir in the cilantro and steamed broccoli florets.
5. Serve the curry over steamed broccoli florets.

Nutrition (per serving): Fat: 15g, Net Carbs: 10g, Protein: 29g, Sodium: 818mg

Tuna & Egg Salad

Prep Time: 10 minutes **Serving:** 4

Ingredients:
- 2 cans of drained Tuna
- 4 hard-boiled eggs, peeled and diced
- 1/2 cup diced celery
- 1/4 cup diced onion
- 2 tablespoons mayonnaise
- 2 tablespoons Dijon mustard
- Salt and pepper to taste
- 4 leaves of lettuce

- 4 slices of whole wheat bread

Directions
1. In a medium mixing bowl, combine the tuna, eggs, celery, and onion.
2. In a separate small mixing bowl, whisk together the mayonnaise and mustard.
3. Add the mayonnaise mixture to the tuna mixture and stir until well combined.
4. Season with salt and pepper to taste.
5. Place a lettuce leaf on each slice of bread.
6. Divide the tuna salad evenly among the bread slices.
7. Serve immediately.

Nutrition (per serving): Fat: 13g, Net Carbs: 20g, Protein: 34g, Sodium: 707mg

Garlic Lemon Shrimp

Prep Time: 10 minutes **Cook time:** 10 minutes **Serving:** 4

Ingredients:
- 1 pound large shrimp, peeled and deveined
- 1 tablespoon olive oil
- 1/4 teaspoon salt
- 1/4 teaspoon black pepper
- 1 tablespoon minced garlic
- 1/4 cup lemon juice
- 1 tablespoon chopped parsley

Directions:
1. Heat a large skillet over medium-high heat. Add the olive oil and shrimp to the skillet and cook for 2-3 minutes on each side, or until the shrimp are pink and cooked through.
2. Remove the shrimp from the skillet and set aside.
3. In the same skillet, add the garlic and cook for 1-2 minutes or until fragrant.
4. Add the lemon juice and bring to a simmer.
5. Add the cooked shrimp back to the skillet and toss to coat with the lemon garlic sauce.
6. Sprinkle with chopped parsley and serve immediately.

Nutrition (per serving): Fat: 12g, Net Carbs: 3g, Protein: 24g, Sodium: 466mg.

Sushi Salad

Prep Time: 30 minutes **Cook time:** 10 minutes **Serving:** 4

Ingredients:
- 4 cups mixed greens
- 8 oz raw tuna, diced
- 1/2 cup cucumber, diced
- 1/4 cup pickled ginger, diced
- 1/4 cup sesame seeds, toasted
- 2 tablespoons rice vinegar
- 1 tablespoon soy sauce
- 1 teaspoon honey
- 1/4 teaspoon sesame oil

Directions:
1. In a large bowl, combine the mixed greens, diced tuna, cucumber, and pickled ginger.

2. In a small bowl, whisk together the rice vinegar, soy sauce, honey, and sesame oil to create the dressing.
3. Pour the dressing over the salad and toss to combine.
4. Sprinkle sesame seeds on top.
5. Serve and enjoy.

Nutrition (per serving): Fat: 13g, Net Carbs: 8g, Protein: 30g, Sodium: 732mg

Marinara Shrimp Zoodles

Prep Time: 10 minutes **Cook time:** 10 minutes **Serving:** 4

Ingredients:
- 1 pound large shrimp, peeled and deveined
- 1 tablespoon olive oil
- 1/4 cup marinara sauce (no sugar added)
- 1/4 teaspoon salt
- 1/4 teaspoon black pepper
- 1 tablespoon chopped fresh basil (optional)
- 4 medium zucchini, spiralized or julienned

Directions:
1. Heat a large skillet over medium-high heat. Add the olive oil and shrimp to the skillet and cook for 2-3 minutes on each side, or until the shrimp are pink and cooked through.
2. Reduce the heat to low and add the marinara sauce, salt, and pepper to the skillet. Stir to coat the shrimp with the sauce.
3. Cook for an additional 2-3 minutes, or until the sauce is heated through.
4. Add the spiralized or julienned zucchini to the skillet and toss with the sauce to combine.
5. Sprinkle with chopped basil, if desired.
6. Serve the shrimp and zoodles with additional marinara sauce on top, if desired.

Nutrition (per serving)**:** Calories: 170, Fat: 5g, Protein: 24g, Carbohydrates: 10g, Fiber: 2g, Sodium: 600mg

Grilled Lime & Garlic Shrimp Salad

Prep Time: 10 minutes **Cook time:** 8 minutes **Serving:** 4

Ingredients:
- 1 pound large shrimp, peeled and deveined
- 1/4 cup lime juice
- 4 cloves garlic, minced
- 1 tablespoon olive oil
- Salt and pepper, to taste
- 4 cups mixed greens
- 1/2 cup cherry tomatoes, halved
- 1/2 cup sliced cucumber
- 1/4 cup chopped red onion
- 1/4 cup chopped fresh cilantro, for garnish

Directions:
1. In a small bowl, whisk together the lime juice, minced garlic, olive oil, salt, and pepper.

2. Place the shrimp in a large resealable bag or shallow dish and pour the marinade over them. Allow the shrimp to marinate for at least 15 minutes (or up to 2 hours) in the refrigerator.
3. Preheat your grill or a grill pan to medium-high heat.
4. Thread the shrimp onto skewers (if using wooden skewers, soak them in water for at least 15 minutes to prevent them from burning).
5. Grill the shrimp for 2-3 minutes on each side, or until they are pink and opaque.
6. In a large bowl, combine the mixed greens, cherry tomatoes, cucumber, and red onion.
7. Divide the salad among four plates and top each with grilled shrimp.
8. Garnish with fresh cilantro and serve.

Nutrition: Fat: 10g, Net Carbs: 10g, Protein: 30g, Sodium: 391mg

Grilled Lemon and Herb Salmon

Prep Time: 10 minutes **Cook time:** 20 minutes **Serving:** 4

Ingredients:
- 4 (6-ounce) salmon fillets
- 1/4 cup fresh lemon juice
- 2 cloves of garlic, minced
- 1 tablespoon fresh thyme leaves
- 1/4 teaspoon salt
- 1/4 teaspoon black pepper

Directions:
1. Preheat the oven to 375F (190C).
2. In a small bowl, whisk together the lemon juice, garlic, thyme, salt, and pepper.
3. Place the salmon fillets in a baking dish and pour the marinade over them.
4. Bake the salmon for 20 minutes or until the fish is cooked through and flakes easily with a fork.
5. Serve the salmon hot, with additional lemon wedges on the side, if desired.

Nutrition (per serving): Calories: 220, Fat: 12g, Protein: 24g, Carbohydrates: 2g, Fiber: 0g, Sodium: 300mg

Grilled Salmon with Cucumber Dill Sauce

Prep Time: 10 minutes **Cook time:** 10 minutes **Serving:** 4

Ingredients:
- 4 (6-ounce) salmon fillets
- 1/4 cup fresh lemon juice
- 2 cloves garlic, minced
- 1/4 cup chopped fresh dill
- 1/4 teaspoon salt
- 1/4 teaspoon black pepper
- 1/2 cup diced cucumber

Directions
1. Preheat the oven to 375F (190C).
2. In a small bowl, whisk together the lemon juice, garlic, dill, salt, and pepper.
3. Place the salmon fillets in a baking dish and pour the marinade over them.
4. Bake the salmon for 20 minutes or until it is cooked through and flakes easily with a fork.
5. While the salmon is baking, mix the diced cucumber with the remaining dill sauce.

6. Serve the salmon with the cucumber dill sauce on top.

Nutrition (per serving): Fat: 8g, Protein: 24g, Carbohydrates: 2g, Sodium: 400mg

Jalapeno Grilled Salmon with Tomato Confit

Prep Time: 15 minutes **Cook time:** 20 minutes **Serving:** 4

Ingredients:
- 4 salmon fillets
- 4 jalapeno peppers, thinly sliced
- 1 pint cherry tomatoes, halved
- 2 cloves garlic, minced
- 1 tablespoon olive oil
- 1/4 cup chopped fresh cilantro
- Salt and pepper to taste

Directions:
1. Preheat oven to 375F (190C).
2. In a small bowl, mix together jalapeno peppers, cherry tomatoes, garlic, olive oil, cilantro, salt and pepper.
3. Place salmon fillets in a baking dish and top with the tomato confit mixture.
4. Bake for about 20 minutes, or until the salmon is fully cooked.
5. Serve the salmon and tomato confit over a bed of rice or with a side of your choice.

Nutrition (per serving): Fat: 12g, Net Carbs: 6g, Protein: 35g, Sodium: 159mg

Egg with Dill, Pepper, and Salmon

Prep Time: 5 minutes **Cook time:** 15 minutes **Serving:** 2

Ingredients:
- 1 large egg
- 1 tsp chopped fresh dill
- Salt and pepper, to taste
- 2 oz smoked salmon
- 1 cup steamed broccoli or green beans (or other green vegetables)

Directions:
1. In a small nonstick skillet, whisk together the egg, dill, salt, and pepper. Cook over medium-low heat, stirring constantly, until the eggs are set.
2. Serve the eggs with the smoked salmon on top and a side of steamed broccoli or green beans.

Nutrition (per serving): Calories: 170, Protein: 17g, Carbohydrates: 3g, Fat: 10g, Fiber: 2g

Lemon Butter Shrimp with Broccoli

Prep Time: 10 minutes **Cook time:** 10 minutes **Serving:** 4

Ingredients:
- 1/2 pound large shrimp, peeled and deveined
- 2 tablespoons butter
- 1 lemon, zested and juiced
- Salt and pepper, to taste
- 2 cups broccoli florets, steamed

Directions:
1. In a large skillet over medium heat, melt the butter.
2. Add the shrimp and cook for 2-3 minutes per side, or until pink and cooked through.
3. Remove the shrimp from the skillet and set aside.
4. Add the lemon zest, lemon juice, salt and pepper to the skillet. Stir until the sauce thickens.
5. Add the cooked shrimp back to the skillet and toss to coat the shrimp in the lemon butter sauce.
6. Serve the shrimp with steamed broccoli on the side.

Nutrition (per serving): Calories: 232, Protein: 27g, Carbohydrates: 7g, Fat: 13g, Fiber: 2g

Baked Cod with Tomato and Feta Salad

Prep Time: 20 minutes **Cook time:** 20 minutes **Serving:** 4

Ingredients:
- 1 pound cod fillets
- 1 pint cherry or grape tomatoes, halved
- 1/2 cup crumbled feta cheese
- 1 tablespoon olive oil
- 2 cloves garlic, minced
- 1/4 cup chopped fresh dill
- 1 lemon, juiced
- Salt and pepper to taste
- 2 cups of steamed green vegetables (broccoli, spinach, asparagus)

Directions:
1. Preheat your oven to 400°F (200°C).
2. Place the cod fillets in a baking dish.
3. In a small bowl, mix together the cherry or grape tomatoes, feta cheese, minced garlic, dill, and lemon juice.
4. Pour the tomato mixture over the cod fillets.
5. Season with salt and pepper to taste.
6. Bake the cod for 20 minutes, or until it is fully cooked and flakes easily with a fork.
7. Serve the baked cod hot, with the tomato and feta mixture spooned over the top and steamed green vegetables on the side.

Nutrition (per serving): Calories: 243, Protein: 30g, Carbohydrates: 5g, Fat: 13g, Fiber: 2g

Grilled Salmon with Vegetable Medley

Prep Time: 10 minutes **Cook time:** 20 minutes **Serving:** 4

Ingredients:
- 4 salmon fillets
- 1/4 teaspoon salt
- 1/4 teaspoon black pepper
- 1 medium zucchini, diced
- 1 medium yellow squash, diced
- 1 medium red bell pepper, diced

- 1 medium onion, diced
- 2 cloves garlic, minced
- 1 teaspoon dried basil
- 1 teaspoon dried oregano

Directions:
1. Preheat a grill to medium-high heat.
2. Season the salmon fillets with salt and pepper.
3. In a large bowl, mix together the zucchini, yellow squash, bell pepper, onion, garlic, basil, and oregano.
4. Grill the salmon for 4-5 minutes per side, or until cooked through.
5. Grill the vegetables for 8-10 minutes or until slightly charred and tender.
6. Serve the grilled salmon with the grilled vegetables on the side.

Nutrition (per serving): Calories: 226, Protein: 33g, Carbohydrates: 10g, Fat: 10g, Fiber: 3g

Chapter 4: Vegetables & Side Dishes

Spinach and Feta Omelette

Prep Time: 30 minutes **Cook time:** 45 minutes **Serving:** 6

Ingredients:
- 2 large eggs
- 1/4 cup baby spinach
- 1/4 cup crumbled feta cheese
- 1/4 cup diced cherry or grape tomatoes
- 1/4 cup diced white onion
- 2 cloves garlic, minced
- Salt and pepper, to taste
- 2 tsp of butter or oil

Directions:
1. Heat a skillet over medium heat and add the butter or oil.
2. Add the minced garlic and diced onion, and sauté until the onion is translucent.
3. Add the spinach to the skillet and cook until it is wilted, about 3-4 minutes.
4. In a separate mixing bowl, beat the eggs together with a fork or whisk.
5. Pour the beaten eggs over the spinach mixture, and let it cook for a minute.
6. Sprinkle diced cherry or grape tomatoes and crumbled feta cheese over the top of the omelette.
7. Season with salt and pepper to taste.
8. Carefully fold the omelette in half, and cook for another 1-2 minutes, or until the eggs are set.
9. Serve immediately

Nutrition (per serving): Calories: 195, Protein: 14g, Carbohydrates: 3g, Fat: 17g, Fiber: 1g

Greek Style Mini Burger Pies

Prep Time: 20 minutes **Cook time:** 30 minutes **Serving:** 4

Ingredients:
- 1 pound ground turkey
- 1/4 cup finely chopped red onion
- 2 cloves garlic, minced
- 1 teaspoon dried oregano
- 1/2 teaspoon salt
- 1/4 teaspoon black pepper
- 2 tablespoons chopped fresh parsley
- 2 tablespoons chopped fresh mint
- 4 cups steamed broccoli
- 4 tablespoons unsalted butter, melted
- Salt and pepper to taste

Directions:
1. Preheat your oven to 375°F (190°C). Line a baking sheet with parchment paper.

2. In a large skillet over medium heat, cook the ground turkey, onion, garlic, oregano, salt, and pepper until the turkey is browned and the vegetables are softened. Drain any excess fat.
3. Stir in the parsley and mint, and remove from heat.
4. To assemble the mini burger pies, take 1/4 cup of the turkey mixture and shape it into a small patty.
5. Place the patty on a baking sheet lined with parchment paper. Repeat to make 4 total patties.
6. Bake the mini burger patties for 20-25 minutes or until cooked through.
7. Serve the cooked mini burger patties with steamed broccoli on the side.

Nutrition (per serving): Calories: 256, Protein: 27g, Carbohydrates: 6g, Fat: 16g, Fiber: 2g

Peanut Butter and Cottage Cheese Dip

Prep Time: 10 minutes **Cook time:** 0 minutes **Serving:** 4

Ingredients:
- 1/4 cup creamy peanut butter
- 1/2 cup non-fat cottage cheese
- 2 tablespoons chopped fresh parsley
- 2 tablespoons chopped fresh mint
- Salt and pepper to taste
- 4 cups of raw vegetables (such as celery, bell peppers, carrots)

Directions:
1. In a blender or food processor, combine the peanut butter, cottage cheese, parsley, mint, salt and pepper.
2. Pulse until well blended and smooth.
3. Serve the dip with raw vegetables for dipping.

Nutrition (per serving): Calories: 131, Protein: 12g, Carbohydrates: 6g, Fat: 8g, Fiber: 2g

Tofu Power Bowl

Prep Time: 20 minutes **Cook time:** 20 minutes **Serving:** 4

Ingredients:
- 1 block firm tofu
- 1 cup cauliflower rice, uncooked
- 1 small head broccoli, cut into florets
- 1 red bell pepper, diced
- 1 carrot, peeled and thinly sliced
- 2 cloves garlic, minced
- 2 tablespoons coconut aminos or soy sauce
- 1 tbsp olive oil
- 1 tbsp rice vinegar
- 1 tsp honey
- Sesame seeds, for garnish

Directions:
1. Press the tofu for at least 15 minutes to remove excess water. Cut the tofu into 1-inch cubes.
2. In a separate pan, heat the olive oil over medium heat. Add the minced garlic and cook for 1 minute.

3. Add the broccoli, bell pepper, and carrot to the pan and cook for 5-7 minutes, or until the vegetables are tender.
4. In a small bowl, whisk together the coconut aminos, rice vinegar, and honey.
5. Add the tofu to the pan with the vegetables and pour the coconut aminos mixture over the top. Toss to coat the tofu and vegetables in the sauce.
6. Cook for an additional 3-5 minutes, or until the tofu is heated through.
7. Serve the tofu and vegetables over the cauliflower rice and sprinkle with sesame seeds. Enjoy!

Nutrition (per serving): Fat: 12g, Net Carbs: 15g, Protein: 29g, Sodium: 437mg

Grilled Veggie Kabobs

Prep Time: 15 minutes **Cook time:** 20 minutes **Serving:** 4

Ingredients:
- 1 red bell pepper, cut into 1-inch pieces
- 1 yellow bell pepper, cut into 1-inch pieces
- 1 orange bell pepper, cut into 1-inch pieces
- 1 small red onion, cut into 1-inch pieces
- 1 small zucchini, sliced into 1/4-inch rounds
- 1 small yellow squash, sliced into 1/4-inch rounds
- 8 cherry tomatoes
- 2 tbsp lemon juice
- 2 cloves garlic, minced
- 1 teaspoon dried basil
- 1/2 teaspoon dried oregano
- 1/4 teaspoon salt
- 1/4 teaspoon black pepper

Directions:
1. Preheat grill to medium-high heat.
2. In a small bowl, whisk together lemon juice, garlic, basil, oregano, salt, and pepper.
3. Thread the bell peppers, onion, zucchini, yellow squash, and cherry tomatoes onto skewers. Brush the skewers with the lemon juice mixture.
4. Place the skewers on the grill and cook for 20 minutes, turning occasionally and brushing with the lemon juice mixture, until vegetables are tender and slightly charred.
5. Serve hot.

Nutrition (per serving): Fat: 2g, Carbohydrates: 20g, Protein: 4g, Sodium: 200mg

Grilled Cauliflower Steaks

Prep Time: 10 minutes **Cook time:** 20 minutes **Serving:** 4

Ingredients:
- Cauliflower
- 1 large head Olive oil
- 1 tablespoon Salt
- 1/4 teaspoon Pepper
- 1/4 teaspoon Lemon juice
- 1 tablespoon Garlic
- 1 clove minced Parsley

- 2 tablespoons chopped

Directions:
1. Preheat your grill to medium-high heat.
2. Cut the cauliflower into 1-inch thick "steaks" by slicing the cauliflower head from the top down through the center. You should be able to get 2-3 steaks from each head of cauliflower.
3. In a small bowl, mix together the olive oil, salt, pepper, lemon juice, minced garlic, and chopped parsley.
4. Brush the mixture onto both sides of the cauliflower steaks.
5. Place the cauliflower steaks on the preheated grill and cook for about 10 minutes on each side, or until tender and grill marks appear.
6. Remove the cauliflower from the grill and serve hot. Enjoy!

Nutrition (per serving): Calories: 95 Fat: 7g Carbohydrates: 9g Protein: 4g Sodium: 240mg

Vegetable Hash with White Beans

Prep Time: 10 minutes **Cook time:** 20 minutes **Serving:** 4

Ingredients:
- Olive oil 1 tablespoon
- Onion
- 1 diced Red bell pepper
- 1 diced Yellow bell pepper
- 1 diced Potatoes
- 2 medium diced Zucchini
- 1 diced Garlic
- 2 cloves minced Canned white beans
- 1 cup drained and rinsed Salt
- 1/4 teaspoon Pepper
- 1/4 teaspoon Parsley
- 2 tablespoons chopped

Directions:
1. Heat the olive oil in a large skillet over medium heat. Add the onion, bell peppers, potatoes, and zucchini to the skillet. Cook for about 10 minutes, or until the vegetables are tender.
2. Add the minced garlic and white beans to the skillet. Cook for an additional 5 minutes.
3. Season the hash with salt and pepper to taste. Garnish with chopped parsley and serve hot. Enjoy!

Nutrition (per serving): Calories: 168 Fat: 5g Carbohydrates: 27g Protein: 6g Sodium: 281mg

Ratatouille

Prep Time: 10 minutes **Cook time:** 45 minutes **Serving:** 4

Ingredients:
- Olive oil, 2 tablespoons
- Onion
- 1 diced Eggplant
- 1 medium diced Zucchini
- 1 diced Yellow squash

- 1 diced Red bell pepper
- 1 diced Tomato
- 1 diced Garlic
- 3 cloves minced Thyme
- 1 teaspoon Basil
- 1 teaspoon Salt
- 1/4 teaspoon Pepper
- 1/4 teaspoon

Directions:
1. Heat 1 tablespoon of olive oil in a large skillet over medium heat. Add the onion, eggplant, zucchini, yellow squash, and bell pepper to the skillet. Cook for about 10 minutes, or until the vegetables are tender.
2. Add the tomato, minced garlic, thyme, and basil to the skillet. Cook for an additional 15 minutes.
3. Season the ratatouille with salt and pepper to taste. Serve hot. Enjoy!

Nutrition (per serving): Calories: 102 Fat: 7g Carbohydrates: 10g Protein: 2g Sodium: 237mg

Grilled Peach and Arugula Salad

Prep Time: 10 minutes **Cook time:** 10 minutes **Serving:** 4

Ingredients:
- 4 peaches, halved and pitted
- 1 tablespoon olive oil
- Salt and pepper, to taste
- 4 cups arugula
- 1/4 cup crumbled feta cheese
- 2 tablespoons apple cider vinegar
- 1 tablespoon honey
- 1 teaspoon Dijon mustard
- 1/4 teaspoon salt
- 1/4 teaspoon black pepper

Directions:
1. Preheat your grill to medium-high heat.
2. Brush the peach halves with olive oil and season with salt and pepper.
3. Grill the peaches for about 5 minutes per side, or until tender and grill marks appear. Remove from grill and allow to cool.
4. In a large bowl, combine the arugula, crumbled feta cheese, and grilled peaches.
5. In a small bowl, whisk together apple cider vinegar, honey, Dijon mustard, salt, and pepper.
6. Drizzle the dressing over the salad and toss to combine.
7. Serve the salad immediately.

Nutrition (per serving): Fat: 10g, Net Carbs: 15g, Protein: 6g, Sodium: 260mg

Stewed Herbed Fruit

Prep Time: 10 minutes **Cook time:** 20 minutes **Serving:** 4

Ingredients:
- 1 tbsp Olive oil
- Apples
- 2 medium diced Pears
- 2 medium diced Cranberries
- 1/2 cup Orange juice
- 2 tbsp Honey
- 1 tsp Thyme
- 1/2 tsp Cinnamon
- Salt and pepper, to taste

Directions:
1. Heat the olive oil in a large saucepan over medium heat. Add the diced apples and pears to the saucepan. Cook for about 5 minutes, or until the fruit is tender.
2. Stir in the cranberries, orange juice, honey, thyme, and cinnamon. Cook for an additional 15 minutes, or until the fruit is fully stewed and the cranberries have burst.
3. Season with salt and pepper to taste.
4. Serve the stewed fruit as a side dish. Enjoy!

Nutrition (per serving): Calories: 120, Fat: 3g, Carbohydrates: 25g, Protein: 1g, Sodium: 10mg

Three-Bean Medley

Prep Time: 10 minutes **Cook time:** 20 minutes **Serving:** 4

Ingredients:
- 1 tablespoon olive oil
- 1 diced onion
- 2 cloves minced garlic
- 1 cup drained and rinsed canned kidney beans
- 1 cup drained and rinsed canned black beans
- 1 cup drained and rinsed canned chickpeas
- 1 cup diced tomatoes
- 1 tablespoon chili powder
- 1 teaspoon cumin
- 1/4 teaspoon salt
- 1/4 teaspoon pepper

Directions:
1. Heat the olive oil in a large saucepan over medium heat. Add the diced onion and minced garlic to the saucepan. Cook for about 5 minutes, or until the onion is translucent.
2. Stir in the kidney beans, black beans, chickpeas, diced tomatoes, chili powder, cumin, salt, and pepper. Cook for an additional 15 minutes, or until the beans are fully heated through.
3. Serve the three-bean medley hot. Enjoy!

Nutrition (per serving): Calories: 149 Fat: 3g Carbohydrates: 21g Protein: 10g Sodium: 435mg

Herbed Garlic Black Beans

Prep Time: 10 minutes **Cook time:** 20 minutes **Serving:** 4

Ingredients:

- Olive oil
- 1 tablespoon Onion
- 1 diced Garlic
- 2 cloves minced Canned black beans
- 2 cups drained and rinsed Lemon juice
- 1 tablespoon Thyme
- 1 teaspoon Basil
- 1 teaspoon Salt
- 1/4 teaspoon Pepper
- 1/4 teaspoon

Directions:
1. Heat the olive oil in a large saucepan over medium heat. Add the diced onion and minced garlic to the saucepan. Cook for about 5 minutes, or until the onion is translucent.
2. Stir in the black beans, lemon juice, thyme, basil, salt, and pepper. Cook for an additional 15 minutes, or until the beans are fully heated through.
3. Serve the herbed garlic black beans hot. Enjoy!

Nutrition (per serving): Calories: 120 Fat: 4g Carbohydrates: 18g Protein: 6g Sodium: 571mg

Cucumber Salad

Prep Time: 10 minutes **Cook time:** 0 minutes **Serving:** 4

Ingredients:
- Cucumber
- 1 large sliced Tomato
- 1 medium diced Red onion
- 1/4 medium thinly sliced Lemon juice
- 2 tablespoons Extra-virgin olive oil
- 1 tablespoon Parsley
- 2 tablespoons chopped Mint
- 2 tablespoons chopped Salt
- 1/4 teaspoon Pepper

Directions:
1. In a large bowl, combine the sliced cucumber, diced tomato, and thinly sliced red onion.
2. In a small bowl, whisk together the lemon juice, olive oil, chopped parsley, and chopped mint. Season the dressing with salt and pepper to taste.
3. Pour the dressing over the cucumber mixture. Toss to coat.
4. Serve the cucumber salad chilled or at room temperature. Enjoy!

Nutrition (per serving): Calories: 72 Fat: 5g Carbohydrates: 8g Protein: 2g Sodium: 172mg

Avocado Chicken Salad

Prep Time: 10 minutes, **Cook time:** 0 minutes, **Serving:** 4

Ingredients:
- Shredded chicken, 2 cups
- Avocado, 1 medium mashed

- Mayonnaise, 2 tablespoons
- Lemon juice, 1 tablespoon
- Cilantro, 2 tablespoons chopped
- Garlic powder, 1/4 teaspoon
- Salt, 1/4 teaspoon
- Pepper, 1/4 teaspoon

Directions:
1. In a large bowl, combine the shredded chicken, mashed avocado, mayonnaise, lemon juice, and chopped cilantro.
2. Season the chicken salad with garlic powder, salt, and pepper. Mix well to combine.
3. Serve the avocado chicken salad chilled or at room temperature. Enjoy!

Nutrition (per serving): Calories: 295, Fat: 21g, Carbohydrates: 6g, Protein: 23g, Sodium: 456mg

High-Protein Salad

Prep Time: 10 minutes **Cook time:** 0 minutes **Serving:** 4

Ingredients:
- Lettuce
- 4 cups Chicken
- 1 cup cooked and diced Egg
- 1 hard-boiled and diced Cheese
- 1/4 cup shredded Peas
- 1/4 cup frozen Carrots
- 1/4 cup grated Sunflower seeds
- 2 tablespoons Dressing of choice

Directions:
1. In a large bowl, combine the lettuce, diced chicken, diced hard-boiled egg, shredded cheese, frozen peas, grated carrots, and sunflower seeds.
2. Serve the high-protein salad with your dressing of choice. Enjoy!

Nutrition (per serving): Calories: 199 Fat: 9g Carbohydrates: 11g Protein: 20g Sodium: 181mg

Apple Strawberry Salad

Prep Time: 10 minutes **Serving:** 4

Ingredients:
- 1 large apple, thinly sliced
- 1 cup strawberries, hulled and sliced
- 1/4 cup slivered almonds
- 1/4 cup crumbled feta cheese
- 1/4 cup diced red onion
- 2 tablespoons lemon juice
- 2 tablespoons olive oil 1 tablespoon honey
- 1/4 teaspoon salt
- 1/4 teaspoon black pepper

Directions:
1. In a large mixing bowl, combine the apple slices, strawberry slices, slivered almonds, feta cheese, and red onion.
2. In a separate small mixing bowl, whisk together the lemon juice, olive oil, honey, salt, and black pepper.
3. Pour the dressing over the fruit and cheese mixture, and toss until everything is evenly coated.
4. Serve the salad immediately, or chill in the refrigerator until ready to serve. Enjoy!

Nutrition (per serving): Calories: 173, Fat: 13g, Carbohydrates: 16g, Protein: 3g, Sodium: 192mg

Spinach Tomato Salad

Prep Time: 5 minutes **Serving:** 4

Ingredients:
- 5 cups baby spinach
- 1 cup cherry tomatoes, halved
- 1/2 cup red onion, thinly sliced
- 1/4 cup olive oil
- 1/4 cup balsamic vinegar
- 1 clove garlic, minced
- 1/4 teaspoon salt
- 1/4 teaspoon black pepper

Directions:
1. In a large mixing bowl, combine the baby spinach, cherry tomatoes, and red onion.
2. In a separate small mixing bowl, whisk together the olive oil, balsamic vinegar, garlic, salt, and black pepper.
3. Pour the dressing over the spinach mixture, and toss until everything is evenly coated.
4. Serve the salad immediately, or chill in the refrigerator until ready to serve. Enjoy!

Nutrition (per serving): Calories: 160, Fat: 14g, Carbohydrates: 10g, Protein: 2g, Sodium: 237mg

Stuffed Avocado

Prep Time: 10 minutes **Serving:** 4

Ingredients:
- 4 avocados
- 1/2 cup cherry tomatoes, diced
- 1/4 cup corn kernels
- 1/4 cup black beans, rinsed and drained
- 1/4 cup diced red onion
- 2 tablespoons chopped fresh cilantro
- 1 tablespoon lime juice
- 1/4 teaspoon salt
- 1/4 teaspoon black pepper

Directions:
1. Cut the avocados in half and remove the pits. Scoop out a small amount of the avocado flesh from the center of each half to create a well.

2. In a small mixing bowl, combine the cherry tomatoes, corn, black beans, red onion, cilantro, lime juice, salt, and black pepper.
3. Divide the mixture evenly among the avocado halves, stuffing it into the wells.
4. Serve the stuffed avocados immediately, or chill in the refrigerator until ready to serve. Enjoy!

Nutrition (per serving): Calories: 213, Fat: 17g, Carbohydrates: 16g, Protein: 4g, Sodium: 214mg

Radish Chips

Prep Time: 10 minutes **Cook time:** 25 minutes **Serving:** 4

Ingredients:
- 1 bunch radishes, thinly sliced
- 1 tablespoon olive oil
- 1/4 teaspoon salt
- 1/4 teaspoon black pepper

Directions:
1. Preheat your oven to 350°F (180°C). Line a baking sheet with parchment paper.
2. In a small mixing bowl, toss the radish slices with the olive oil, salt, and black pepper.
3. Spread the radish slices in a single layer on the prepared baking sheet.
4. Bake for 20-25 minutes, or until the radish slices are crisp and golden brown.
5. Serve the radish chips immediately, or store in an airtight container for up to 3 days. Enjoy!

Nutrition (per serving): Calories: 46, Fat: 3g, Carbohydrates: 5g, Protein: 1g, Sodium: 177mg

Cilantro Lime Yogurt Dip

Prep Time: 10 minutes **Serving:** 4

Ingredients:
- 1 cup plain Greek yogurt
- 1 avocado, peeled and pitted
- 1/4 cup chopped cilantro
- 2 tablespoons lime juice
- 1 clove garlic, minced
- 1/4 teaspoon salt
- 1/4 teaspoon black pepper

Directions:
1. In a blender or food processor, combine the Greek yogurt, avocado, cilantro, lime juice, garlic, salt, and black pepper.
2. Blend until the mixture is smooth and creamy.
3. Transfer the dip to a serving dish, and serve immediately or chill in the refrigerator until ready to serve.
4. Enjoy!

Nutrition (per serving): Calories: 110, Fat: 7g, Carbohydrates: 7g, Protein: 7g, Sodium: 120mg.

Chapter 5: Soup Recipes

Black Bean Soup

Prep Time: 10 minutes **Cook time:** 30 minutes **Serving:** 4

Ingredients:
- 1 tablespoon olive oil
- 1 medium onion, diced
- 2 cloves garlic, minced
- 1 jalapeño pepper, seeded and minced
- 1 teaspoon ground cumin
- 1 teaspoon ground coriander
- 1/2 teaspoon smoked paprika
- 1/4 teaspoon salt
- 1/4 teaspoon black pepper
- 1 can (14.5 ounces) diced tomatoes, undrained
- 1 can (14.5 ounces) black beans, rinsed and drained
- 1 can (14.5 ounces) chicken broth
- 1/4 cup chopped fresh cilantro

Directions:
1. In a large pot, heat the olive oil over medium heat. Add the onion, garlic, and jalapeño pepper, and cook until the vegetables are soft and fragrant, about 5 minutes.
2. Stir in the cumin, coriander, paprika, salt, and black pepper, and cook for 1 minute more.
3. Add the tomatoes, black beans, and chicken broth to the pot. Bring the mixture to a boil, then reduce the heat to low and simmer for 30 minutes.
4. Using an immersion blender, blend the soup until it is smooth and creamy. Alternatively, you can transfer the soup in batches to a blender or food processor and blend until smooth.
5. Return the soup to the pot and heat through. Stir in the cilantro.

Nutrition (per serving): Calories: 156, Fat: 5g, Carbohydrates: 20g, Protein: 9g, Sodium: 612mg

Vegetable and Lentil Soup

Prep Time: 10 minutes **Cook time:** 30 minutes **Serving:** 4

Ingredients:
- 1 tablespoon olive oil
- 1 medium onion, diced
- 2 cloves garlic, minced
- 1 cup diced zucchini
- 1 cup diced celery
- 1/2 cup green lentils
- 1 can (14.5 ounces) diced tomatoes, undrained
- 4 cups vegetable broth
- 1 teaspoon dried thyme

- 1/2 teaspoon salt
- 1/4 teaspoon black pepper

Directions:
1. In a large pot, heat the olive oil over medium heat. Add the onion, garlic, zucchini, celery and cook until the vegetables are soft and fragrant, about 5 minutes.
2. Stir in the lentils, diced tomatoes, vegetable broth, thyme, salt, and black pepper. Bring the mixture to a boil, then reduce the heat to low and simmer for 20-25 minutes, or until the lentils and vegetables are tender.
3. Serve the soup hot, garnished with fresh herbs if desired. Enjoy!

Nutrition (per serving): Calories: 149, Fat: 5g, Carbohydrates: 18g, Protein: 8g, Sodium: 880mg

Broccoli Blue Cheese

Prep Time: 10 minutes **Cook time:** 10 minutes **Serving:** 4

Ingredients:
- 1 pound broccoli florets
- 1 tablespoon olive oil
- 1/4 teaspoon salt
- 1/4 teaspoon black pepper
- 1/4 cup crumbled blue cheese

Directions:
1. Preheat your oven to 400°F (200°C). Line a baking sheet with parchment paper.
2. In a small mixing bowl, toss the broccoli florets with the olive oil, salt, and black pepper.
3. Spread the broccoli in a single layer on the prepared baking sheet.
4. Roast the broccoli for 8-10 minutes, or until it is tender and caramelized.
5. Sprinkle the crumbled blue cheese over the broccoli, and roast for 2 minutes more, or until the cheese is melted and bubbly.
6. Serve the broccoli hot, garnished with additional blue cheese if desired. Enjoy!

Nutrition (per serving): Calories: 82, Fat: 6g, Carbohydrates: 6g, Protein: 4g, Sodium: 267mg

Mushroom and Spinach Soup

Prep Time: 10 minutes **Cook time:** 20 minutes **Serving:** 4

Ingredients:
- 1 tablespoon olive oil
- 1 onion, diced
- 8 oz mushrooms, sliced
- 2 cloves garlic, minced
- 4 cups vegetable broth
- 2 cups spinach leaves
- 1/4 teaspoon salt
- 1/4 teaspoon black pepper

Directions:

1. In a large pot, heat the olive oil over medium heat. Add the onion, mushrooms, and garlic and cook until the vegetables are soft and fragrant, about 5 minutes.
2. Stir in the vegetable broth, bring to a simmer and cook for 15 minutes.
3. Add the spinach leaves and cook for an additional 5 minutes.
4. Season with salt and pepper to taste.
5. Use an immersion blender to blend the soup until smooth.
6. Serve hot and enjoy!

Nutrition (per serving): Calories: 63, Fat: 4g, Carbohydrates: 7g, Protein: 3g, Sodium: 589mg

Cold Cauliflower-Coconut Soup

Prep Time: 20 minutes **Cook time:** 20 minutes **Serving:** 4

Ingredients:
- Cauliflower
- 1 head Coconut milk
- 1 can (13.5 ounces) Chicken broth
- 4 cups Cilantro
- 1/4 cup Lime
- 1 Jalapeno pepper
- 1/2 Garlic
- 2 cloves Salt
- 1/2 teaspoon Pepper
- 1/4 teaspoon

Directions:
1. Cut the cauliflower into small florets and set aside.
2. In a large pot, combine the chicken broth, coconut milk, cilantro, jalapeno pepper, garlic, salt, and pepper. Bring to a boil.
3. Add the cauliflower to the pot and reduce the heat to a simmer. Cook for 15-20 minutes or until the cauliflower is tender.
4. Using an immersion blender, blend the soup until it is smooth and creamy. If you do not have an immersion blender, you can transfer the soup to a blender and blend until smooth.
5. Squeeze in the juice of the lime and stir to combine.
6. Serve the soup cold and garnish with additional cilantro and a slice of lime if desired. Enjoy!

Nutrition (per serving): Fat: 12g, Net Carbs: 18g, Protein: 7g, Sodium: 628mg

Cream of Broccoli & Cauliflower Soup

Prep Time: 15 minutes **Cook time:** 25 minutes **Serving:** 4

Ingredients:
- 1 head broccoli, cut into small florets
- 1 head cauliflower, cut into small florets
- 1 onion, diced
- 3 cloves garlic, minced
- 4 cups chicken broth

- 1/4 cup heavy cream
- 2 tablespoons olive oil
- Salt and pepper to taste

Directions:
1. In a large pot, heat the olive oil over medium heat. Add the onion and garlic, and sauté until the onion is translucent, about 5 minutes.
2. Add the broccoli, cauliflower, chicken broth, salt, and pepper to the pot. Bring to a boil and then reduce the heat to a simmer. Cook for 20-25 minutes or until the vegetables are tender.
3. Using an immersion blender, blend the soup until it is smooth and creamy. If you do not have an immersion blender, you can transfer the soup to a blender and blend until smooth.
4. Stir in the heavy cream and heat the soup until it is hot and well combined.
5. Serve the soup hot and garnish with additional cream and pepper if desired.

Nutrition (per serving): Calories: 120, Fat: 8g, Carbohydrates: 10g, Protein: 4g, Sodium: 638mg

Cold Tomato Summer Vegetable Soup

Prep Time: 20 minutes **Cook time:** 0 minutes **Serving:** 4

Ingredients:
- Tomatoes
- 4 Cucumber
- 1 Red bell pepper
- 1 Yellow bell pepper
- 1 Green bell pepper
- 1 Red onion, 1/2 Garlic
- 2 cloves Basil
- 1/4 cup Olive oil
- 2 tablespoons Red wine vinegar
- 2 tablespoons Salt
- 1/2 teaspoon Pepper
- 1/4 teaspoon

Directions:
1. Dice the tomatoes, cucumber, bell peppers, and red onion into small pieces. Mince the garlic and chop the basil.
2. In a large mixing bowl, combine the diced vegetables, minced garlic, chopped basil, olive oil, red wine vinegar, salt, and pepper. Stir until the vegetables are evenly coated.
3. Chill the soup in the refrigerator for at least 1 hour to allow the flavors to meld.
4. Serve the soup cold, garnished with additional basil if desired. Enjoy!

Nutrition (per serving): Fat: 14g, Net Carbs: 18g, Protein: 4g, Sodium: 358mg

Spinach and Coconut Milk Soup

Prep Time: 10 minutes **Cook time:** 20 minutes **Serving:** 4

Ingredients:
- 1 tablespoon olive oil

- 1 medium onion, diced
- 2 cloves garlic, minced
- 1 teaspoon ground cumin
- 1/4 teaspoon salt
- 1/4 teaspoon black pepper
- 1 can (14 ounces) coconut milk
- 4 cups chicken broth
- 4 cups baby spinach

Directions:
1. In a large pot, heat the olive oil over medium heat. Add the onion and garlic and cook until softened, about 5 minutes.
2. Stir in the cumin, salt, and pepper and cook for 1 minute more.
3. Add the coconut milk, chicken broth and spinach, bring the mixture to a boil then reduce the heat to low and simmer for 15-20 minutes.
4. Using an immersion blender, blend the soup until it is smooth and creamy. If you do not have an immersion blender, you can transfer the soup to a blender and blend until smooth.
5. Serve the soup hot, garnished with additional spinach leaves if desired. Enjoy!

Nutrition (per serving): Calories: 140, Fat: 11g, Carbohydrates: 9g, Protein: 4g, Sodium: 587mg

Alkaline Carrot and Mushroom Soup

Prep Time: 15 minutes **Cook time:** 30 minutes **Serving:** 4

Ingredients:
- 1 lb. carrots, peeled and sliced
- 8 oz. mushrooms, sliced
- 1 medium onion, diced
- 2 cloves of garlic, minced
- 4 cups of low-sodium vegetable broth
- 1/2 cup of unsweetened coconut milk
- 1 tbsp. grated ginger
- 1 tbsp. lemon juice
- Salt and pepper to taste

Directions:
1. In a large pot, heat some oil over medium heat. Add the onion and garlic and sauté until the onion is translucent, about 5 minutes.
2. Add the carrots, mushrooms, vegetable broth, grated ginger, salt, and pepper to the pot. Bring to a boil and then reduce the heat to a simmer. Cook for 25-30 minutes or until the carrots are tender.
3. Using an immersion blender, blend the soup until it is smooth and creamy. If you do not have an immersion blender, you can transfer the soup to a blender and blend until smooth.
4. Stir in the coconut milk and lemon juice.
5. Serve the soup hot and garnish with additional lemon wedges and sliced mushrooms if desired. Enjoy!

Nutrition (per serving): Calories: 104, Fat: 5g, Carbohydrates: 12g, Protein: 4g, Sodium: 392mg

Lean Green Cauliflower Soup

Prep Time: 15 minutes **Cook time:** 25 minutes **Serving:** 4

Ingredients:

- 1 head cauliflower
- 1 onion, diced
- 3 cloves garlic, minced
- 4 cups vegetable broth
- 1 cup low-fat milk or non-dairy milk
- 1/4 cup grated Parmesan cheese
- 1 tablespoon olive oil
- 1/2 teaspoon salt
- 1/4 teaspoon black pepper

Directions:

1. Cut the cauliflower into small florets and set aside. Dice the onion and mince the garlic.
2. In a large pot, heat olive oil over medium heat. Add the onion and garlic and sauté until the onion is translucent, about 5 minutes.
3. Add the cauliflower, vegetable broth, salt, and pepper to the pot. Bring to a boil and then reduce the heat to a simmer. Cook for 20-25 minutes or until the cauliflower is tender.
4. Using an immersion blender, blend the soup until it is smooth and creamy. If you do not have an immersion blender, you can transfer the soup to a blender and blend until smooth.
5. Stir in the low-fat milk or non-dairy milk and grated Parmesan cheese and heat the soup until it is hot and well combined.
6. Serve the soup hot and garnish with additional grated cheese if desired. Enjoy!

Nutrition (per serving): Fat: 5g, Net Carbs: 14g, Protein: 7g, Sodium: 579mg

Chilled Avocado Tomato Soup

Prep Time: 15 minutes **Cook time:** 0 minutes **Serving:** 4

Ingredients:

- 2 ripe avocados
- 2 ripe tomatoes
- 4 small cucumbers
- 1/2 red onion
- 2 cloves of garlic
- 1/4 cup fresh basil leaves
- 2 tablespoons lime juice
- 2 tablespoons red wine vinegar
- 1/2 teaspoon salt
- 1/4 teaspoon black pepper

Directions:

1. Dice the avocados, tomatoes, cucumbers, and red onion into small pieces. Mince the garlic and chop the basil.
2. In a large mixing bowl, combine the diced vegetables, minced garlic, chopped basil, lime juice, red wine vinegar, salt, and pepper. Stir until the vegetables are evenly coated.
3. Chill the soup in the refrigerator for at least 1 hour to allow the flavors to meld.
4. Serve the soup cold, garnished with additional basil if desired. Enjoy!

Nutrition (per serving): Fat: 6g, Net Carbs: 20g, Protein: 4g, Sodium: 358mg

Pumpkin and White Bean Soup with Sage

Prep Time: 15 minutes **Cook time:** 30 minutes **Serving:** 4

Ingredients:
- Pumpkin
- 1 (about 2 pounds) White beans
- 1 can (15 ounces) Onion
- 1 Garlic
- 3 cloves Vegetable broth
- 4 cups Skim milk
- 1 cup Sage
- 1 tablespoon Olive oil
- 2 tablespoons Salt
- 1/2 teaspoon Pepper

Directions:
1. Peel and chop the pumpkin into small pieces. Dice the onion and mince the garlic.
2. In a large pot, heat the olive oil over medium heat. Add the onion and garlic and sauté until the onion is translucent, about 5 minutes.
3. Add the pumpkin, white beans, vegetable broth, salt, and pepper to the pot. Bring to a boil and then reduce the heat to a simmer. Cook for 25-30 minutes or until the pumpkin is tender.
4. Using an immersion blender, blend the soup until it is smooth and creamy. If you do not have an immersion blender, you can transfer the soup to a blender and blend until smooth.
5. Stir in the skim milk and chopped sage and heat the soup until it is hot and well combined.
6. Serve the soup hot and garnish with additional sage if desired. Enjoy!

Nutrition (per serving): Fat: 4g, Net Carbs: 23g, Protein: 11g, Sodium: 639mg

Italian Chicken and Vegetable Soup

Prep Time: 15 minutes **Cook time:** 30 minutes **Serving:** 4

Ingredients: Chicken breasts
- 4 oz boneless, skinless chicken breast, cut into small pieces
- 1 medium onion, diced
- 1 cup diced carrots
- 1 cup diced celery
- 2 cloves garlic, minced
- 1 can (14.5 oz) diced tomatoes
- 1 teaspoon Italian seasoning
- 4 cups chicken broth
- 1 cup chopped spinach
- Salt and pepper to taste

Directions:
1. In a large pot, heat some oil over medium heat. Add the onion, carrots, celery, and garlic, and sauté until the vegetables are tender, about 5 minutes.

2. Add the chicken, tomatoes, Italian seasoning, chicken broth, salt, and pepper to the pot. Bring to a boil and then reduce the heat to a simmer. Cook for 20-25 minutes or until the chicken is cooked through.
3. Stir in the chopped spinach and cook until wilted.
4. Serve the soup hot and garnish with additional Italian seasoning if desired. Enjoy!

Nutrition: Fat: 5g, Net Carbs: 11g, Protein: 20g, Sodium: 624mg

Slow Cooked Lentil Soup

Prep Time: 10 minutes **Cook time:** 2 hours **Serving:** 6

Ingredients:
- 1 cup lentils
- 1 cup onion
- 1 carrot
- 2 celery
- 2 stalks garlic
- 3 cloves tomatoes
- 2 bay leaf
- 1 thyme
- 1 teaspoon chicken broth
- 4 cups water
- 1 tablespoon olive oil
- Salt and pepper to taste

Directions:
1. Rinse the lentils and set aside. Dice the onion, carrots, and celery. Mince the garlic and chop the tomatoes.
2. In a large pot, heat the olive oil over medium heat. Add the onion, carrots, celery, and garlic and sauté until the vegetables are tender, about 5 minutes.
3. Add the lentils, tomatoes, bay leaf, thyme, chicken broth, water, salt, and pepper to the pot. Bring to a boil and then reduce the heat to a simmer. Cook for 1 1/2-2 hours or until the lentils are tender.
4. Remove the bay leaf and serve the soup hot. Garnish with additional thyme if desired. Enjoy!

Nutrition (per serving): Fat: 2.5g, Net Carbs: 8g, Protein: 12g, Sodium: 740mg

Healthy Minestrone Soup

Prep Time: 20 minutes **Cook time:** 45 minutes **Serving:** 8

Ingredients:
- 1 tablespoon olive oil
- 1 onion
- 1 carrot
- 2 celeries
- 2 stalks garlic
- 1 zucchini
- 1 cup green beans
- 1 cup diced tomatoes
- 4 cups chicken or vegetable broth

- 1 cup water
- 1 tablespoon Italian seasoning
- 1 teaspoon salt
- 1/2 teaspoon pepper
- 1/4 teaspoon small pasta
- 1/2 cup cooked white beans or chickpeas

Directions:
1. Heat the olive oil in a large pot over medium heat. Dice the onion, carrots, and celery. Mince the garlic. Slice the zucchini and cut the green beans into 1-inch pieces.
2. Add the onion, carrots, celery, and garlic to the pot and sauté until the vegetables are tender, about 5 minutes.
3. Add the zucchini, green beans, diced tomatoes, broth, water, Italian seasoning, salt, and pepper to the pot. Bring to a boil and then reduce the heat to a simmer.
4. Cook for 30 minutes or until the vegetables are tender.
5. Add the pasta and white beans or chickpeas to the pot and cook for an additional 10-15 minutes or until the pasta is tender.
6. Serve the soup hot and enjoy!

Nutrition (per serving): Fat: 3g, Net Carbs: 18g, Protein: 10g, Sodium: 723mg

Chicken Kohlrabi Noodles Soup

Prep Time: 15 minutes **Cook time:** 45 minutes **Serving:** 4

Ingredients:
- 1 pound chicken breasts
- 1 medium kohlrabi, peeled and spiralized or thinly sliced 1 medium yellow onion diced
- 2 cloves garlic, minced
- 1 quart chicken broth
- 1 teaspoon paprika
- 1/2 teaspoon cumin
- 1/4 teaspoon coriander
- 1/4 teaspoon chili flakes
- 1/4 teaspoon turmeric
- 1/2 teaspoon salt
- 1/4 teaspoon pepper
- 2 tablespoons olive oil

Directions:
1. In a large pot or Dutch oven, heat the olive oil over medium heat.
2. Add the onion and cook until translucent, about 5 minutes.
3. Add the garlic and cook for an additional minute.
4. Add the chicken to the pot and cook until no longer pink, about 5 minutes.
5. Add the kohlrabi, paprika, cumin, coriander, chili flakes, turmeric, salt, and pepper to the pot and stir to combine.
6. Pour in the chicken broth and bring to a boil.
7. Reduce the heat to a simmer and let cook for 30 minutes.

8. Using a fork or tongs, shred the chicken in the pot.
9. Serve hot and enjoy!

Nutrition (per serving): Fat: 12g, Net Carbs: 14g, Protein: 28g, Sodium: 880mg

Curry Roasted Cauliflower Soup

Prep Time: 10 minutes **Cook time:** 40 minutes **Serving:** 4

Ingredients:
- 1 head cauliflower, chopped
- 1 medium yellow onion, diced
- 2 cloves garlic, minced
- 4 cups vegetable broth
- 1/2 cup water
- 1 tablespoon curry powder
- 1 teaspoon paprika
- 1/2 teaspoon cumin
- 1/4 teaspoon coriander
- 1/4 teaspoon chili flakes
- 1/4 teaspoon turmeric
- 1/2 teaspoon salt
- 1/4 teaspoon pepper
- 1 tablespoons olive oil
- 4 oz of lean protein (chicken, turkey, fish, tofu)

Directions:
1. In a large pot or Dutch oven, heat the olive oil over medium heat.
2. Add the onion and cook until translucent, about 5 minutes.
3. Add the garlic and cook for an additional minute.
4. Add the cauliflower, curry powder, paprika, cumin, coriander, chili flakes, turmeric, salt, and pepper to the pot and stir to combine.
5. Pour in the vegetable broth and water and bring to a boil.
6. Reduce the heat to a simmer and let cook for 30 minutes.
7. Add 4 oz of lean protein of your choice.
8. Using an immersion blender, blend the soup until smooth.
9. Serve hot and enjoy!

Nutrition (per serving): Fat: 12g, Net Carbs: 14g, Protein: 20g, Sodium: 840mg

Spicy Zucchini Soup

Prep Time: 10 minutes **Cook time:** 30 minutes **Serving:** 4

Ingredients:
- 1 lb zucchini, diced
- 1 medium onion, diced
- 2 cloves garlic, minced
- 1 teaspoon cumin

- 1/2 teaspoon smoked paprika
- 1/4 teaspoon chili powder
- 1/4 teaspoon cayenne pepper
- 1/4 teaspoon turmeric
- 1/2 teaspoon salt
- 1/4 teaspoon pepper
- 2 tablespoons olive oil
- 4 cups vegetable broth
- 1 cup coconut milk

Directions:
1. In a large pot or Dutch oven, heat the olive oil over medium heat.
2. Add the onion and cook until translucent, about 5 minutes.
3. Add the garlic and cook for an additional minute.
4. Add the zucchini, cumin, smoked paprika, chili powder, cayenne pepper, turmeric, salt, and pepper to the pot and stir to combine.
5. Pour in the vegetable broth and coconut milk and bring to a boil.
6. Reduce the heat to a simmer and let cook for 20-25 minutes or until the zucchini is tender.
7. Using an immersion blender, blend the soup until smooth.
8. Serve hot and enjoy!

Nutrition (per serving): Fat: 18g, Net Carbs: 12g, Protein: 4g, Sodium: 890mg

Egg Drop Soup

Prep Time: 5 minutes **Cook time:** 15 minutes **Serving:** 4

Ingredients:
- 4 cups chicken broth
- 1/2 cup frozen peas and carrots
- 2 green onions, diced
- 2 eggs, beaten
- 1 teaspoon sesame oil
- 1/2 teaspoon salt
- 1/4 teaspoon white pepper

Directions:
1. In a large pot or Dutch oven, bring the chicken broth to a boil over medium-high heat.
2. Add the peas and carrots and green onions to the pot and cook for 3 minutes.
3. In a small mixing bowl, whisk together the eggs, sesame oil, salt, and white pepper.
4. Slowly pour the egg mixture into the pot while stirring the soup in a circular motion.
5. Cook for an additional 2 minutes or until the eggs are fully cooked.
6. Serve hot and enjoy!

Nutrition (per serving): Fat: 6g, Net Carbs: 9g, Protein: 13g, Sodium: 1020mg

Meatball Soup

Prep Time: 10 minutes **Cook time:** 30 minutes **Serving:** 4

Ingredients:
- 1 pound ground turkey
- 1/2 cup bread crumbs
- 1 egg white
- 1/4 cup grated Parmesan cheese
- 1 tablespoon Italian seasoning
- 1/2 teaspoon salt
- 1/4 teaspoon pepper
- 1 medium yellow onion, diced
- 2 cloves garlic, minced
- 4 cups chicken broth
- 1 cup water
- 1 can diced tomatoes
- 1 cup diced carrots
- 1 cup diced celery
- 1 cup diced zucchini
- 1 cup diced mushrooms

Directions:
1. In a large mixing bowl, combine the ground turkey, bread crumbs, egg white, Parmesan cheese, Italian seasoning, salt, and pepper.
2. Form the mixture into small meatballs.
3. In a large pot or Dutch oven, heat some oil over medium heat.
4. Add the meatballs to the pot and cook until browned on all sides, about 5 minutes.
5. Remove the meatballs from the pot and set aside.
6. In the same pot, add the onion and cook until translucent, about 5 minutes.
7. Add the garlic and cook for an additional minute.
8. Add the chicken broth, water, diced tomatoes, diced carrots, diced celery, diced zucchini and diced mushrooms to the pot and bring to a boil.
9. Add the meatballs to the pot and cook for 10-12 minutes or until the vegetables are tender.
10. Serve hot and enjoy!

Nutrition (per serving): Fat: 10g, Net Carbs: 15g, Protein: 28g, Sodium: 1230mg

Spinach and Lentil Soup

Prep Time: 10 minutes **Cook time:** 30 minutes **Serving:** 4

Ingredients:
- 1 tablespoon of olive oil
- 1/2 cup of diced onion
- 1/2 cup of diced carrot
- 1/2 cup of diced celery
- 2 cloves of minced garlic
- 1 cup of green lentils, rinsed and drained
- 4 cups of chicken broth or vegetable broth
- 2 cups of fresh spinach leaves, washed and chopped
- Salt and pepper, to taste

Directions:

1. In a large pot, heat the olive oil over medium heat.
2. Add the onion, carrot, celery, and garlic. Sauté for 2-3 minutes until the vegetables are soft.
3. Add the lentils and broth to the pot and bring to a boil.
4. Reduce the heat and let the soup simmer for 20-25 minutes, or until the lentils are tender.
5. Stir in the chopped spinach leaves and let the soup simmer for an additional 2-3 minutes.
6. Season with salt and pepper to taste.
7. Serve the soup in bowls and enjoy!

Nutrition (per serving): Calories: 174, Protein: 12g, Fat: 4g, Carbohydrates: 22g, Fiber: 8g, Sugar: 3g

Broccoli and Cheddar Soup

Prep Time: 10 minutes **Cook time:** 20 minutes **Serving:** 4

Ingredients:

- 2 tablespoons of butter
- 1/2 cup of diced onion
- 1/2 cup of diced celery
- 2 cloves of minced garlic
- 2 cups of broccoli florets
- 3 cups of chicken broth
- 1 cup of shredded cheddar cheese
- Salt and pepper, to taste
- 1/4 cup of chopped fresh parsley

Directions:

1. In a large pot, melt the butter over medium heat.
2. Add the onion, celery, and garlic. Sauté for 2-3 minutes until the vegetables are soft.
3. Add the broccoli and broth to the pot and bring to a boil.
4. Reduce the heat and let the soup simmer for 10-15 minutes, or until the broccoli is tender.
5. Remove the pot from the heat and use a blender or immersion blender to blend the soup until smooth.
6. Return the pot to the heat and stir in the shredded cheddar cheese until melted.
7. Season with salt and pepper to taste.
8. Garnish with chopped parsley and serve.

Nutrition (per serving): Calories: 174, Protein: 12g, Fat: 4g, Carbohydrates: 22g, Fiber: 8g, Sugar: 3g

Chapter 6: Snack Recipes

Roasted Zucchini Boats with Ground Beef

Prep Time: 10 minutes **Cook time:** 30 minutes **Serving:** 4

Ingredients:

- 2 medium zucchinis
- 1 pound ground turkey
- 1 medium yellow onion, diced
- 2 cloves garlic, minced
- 1 teaspoon Italian seasoning
- 1/2 teaspoon salt
- 1/4 teaspoon pepper
- 1 cup marinara sauce (low sodium)
- 1 cup grated part-skim mozzarella cheese
- 2 cups of chopped spinach or other leafy greens

Directions:

1. Preheat your oven to 400°F (200°C).
2. Cut the zucchinis in half lengthwise and scoop out the seeds.
3. In a large skillet, cook the ground turkey over medium heat until browned, about 5-7 minutes.
4. Add the onion, garlic, Italian seasoning, salt, and pepper to the skillet and cook for an additional 3 minutes.
5. Stir in the marinara sauce and cook for 2 more minutes.
6. Add the spinach or other leafy greens and cook until wilted.
7. Divide the ground turkey mixture among the zucchini boats and top with the mozzarella cheese.
8. Place the zucchini boats on a baking sheet and bake in the preheated oven for 15-20 minutes or until the cheese is melted and bubbly.
9. Serve hot and enjoy!

Nutrition (per serving): Fat: 12g, Net Carbs: 13g, Protein: 32g, Sodium: 540mg

Pumpkin Protein Balls

Prep Time: 10 minutes **Cook time:** 0 minutes **Serving:** 12

Ingredients:

- 1 cup canned pumpkin puree
- 1/2 cup vanilla protein powder
- 1/4 cup almond flour
- 1/4 cup honey
- 1 teaspoon vanilla extract
- 1/2 teaspoon ground cinnamon
- 1/4 teaspoon ground ginger
- 1/4 teaspoon ground nutmeg

- 1/4 teaspoon ground allspice

Directions:
1. In a medium mixing bowl, combine the pumpkin puree, protein powder, almond flour, honey, vanilla extract, cinnamon, ginger, nutmeg, and allspice.
2. Mix until well combined and roll the mixture into small balls.
3. Place the balls on a parchment paper-lined baking sheet and refrigerate for at least 30 minutes.
4. Once chilled, the balls are ready to eat and can be stored in the refrigerator for up to a week.

Nutrition (per serving): Fat: 6g, Net Carbs: 14g, Protein: 8g, Sodium: 60mg

Easy Chicken Curry

Prep Time: 10 minutes **Cook time:** 20 minutes **Serving:** 4

Ingredients:
- 1 pound boneless, skinless chicken breast, cut into bite-sized pieces
- 1 tablespoon olive oil
- 1 medium yellow onion, diced
- 2 cloves garlic, minced
- 1 tablespoon curry powder
- 1 teaspoon ground cumin
- 1/2 teaspoon ground coriander
- 1/4 teaspoon salt
- 1 cup chicken broth
- 1 cup frozen green beans
- 1/2 cup chopped cilantro
- 1 tbsp fat-free Greek yogurt

Directions:
1. In a large skillet, heat the olive oil over medium heat.
2. Add the chicken, onion, and garlic to the skillet and cook until the chicken is no longer pink, about 5-7 minutes.
3. Add the curry powder, cumin, coriander, and salt to the skillet and cook for an additional minute.
4. Stir in the chicken broth and green beans.
5. Bring the mixture to a boil, reduce the heat to low, and simmer for 10 minutes or until the sauce has thickened.
6. Stir in the cilantro and a tablespoon of fat-free Greek yogurt. Serve hot with a side of steamed vegetables.

Nutrition (per serving): Calories: 300, Protein: 27g, Fat: 12g, Carbohydrates: 13g, Fiber: 3g

Spiced Popcorn

Prep Time: 5 minutes **Cook time:** 5 minutes **Serving:** 4

Ingredients:
- 1/4 cup popcorn kernels
- 1 tablespoon olive oil or melted butter
- 1/2 teaspoon chili powder
- 1/4 teaspoon ground cumin

- 1/4 teaspoon ground coriander
- 1/4 teaspoon paprika
- 1/4 teaspoon garlic powder
- 1/4 teaspoon salt

Directions:
1. In a large pot, heat the olive oil or melted butter over medium heat.
2. Add the popcorn kernels to the pot and cover with a lid.
3. Shake the pot occasionally to help the kernels pop evenly.
4. Once the popping has slowed down, remove the pot from the heat and let it sit for a minute to let any remaining kernels pop.
5. In a small mixing bowl, combine the chili powder, cumin, coriander, paprika, garlic powder, and salt.
6. Sprinkle the spice mixture over the popcorn and toss to coat.
7. Serve the spiced popcorn hot and enjoy!

Nutrition (per serving): Fat: 10g, Net Carbs: 6g, Protein: 3g, Sodium: 250mg

Snickerdoodle Pecans

Prep Time: 5 minutes **Cook time:** 20 minutes **Serving:** 4

Ingredients:
- 1 cup pecan halves
- 1 tablespoon erythritol or any other low-carb sweetener
- 1 tablespoon ground cinnamon
- 1/4 teaspoon salt

Directions:
1. Preheat the oven to 350°F (175°C). Line a baking sheet with parchment paper.
2. In a small mixing bowl, combine the erythritol, cinnamon, and salt.
3. Add the pecan halves to the bowl and toss to coat.
4. Spread the pecans on the prepared baking sheet.
5. Bake the pecans for 20 minutes, stirring every 5 minutes.
6. Remove the pecans from the oven and let them cool completely before serving.

Nutrition (per serving): Fat: 20g, Net Carbs: 4g, Protein: 3g, Sodium: 140mg

Almond-Stuffed Dates

Prep Time: 10 minutes **Cook time:** 0 minutes **Serving:** 6

Ingredients:
- 12 large dates
- 12 walnuts
- 4 ounces cream cheese
- 2 tablespoons sugar-free maple syrup

Directions:
1. Carefully slice each date down the center, making sure not to cut all the way through.
2. Stuff each date with a walnut and a small spoonful of cream cheese.
3. Place the stuffed dates on a plate.

4. Drizzle the sugar-free maple syrup over the stuffed dates.
5. Serve the dates cold.

Nutrition (per serving): Fat: 15g, Net Carbs: 10g, Protein: 3g, Sodium: 80mg

Peanut Butter Energy Bites

Prep Time: 10 minutes **Cook time:** 0 minutes **Serving:** 15-20 bites

Ingredients:
- 2 tablespoons smooth peanut butter
- 1/2 cup honey or maple syrup
- 1 cup old-fashioned oats
- 1/4 cup ground flaxseed (optional)
- 1 tsp vanilla extract

Directions:
1. In a medium mixing bowl, combine the peanut butter and honey or maple syrup. Mix until well combined and smooth.
2. Add the oats, chocolate chips, ground flaxseed (if using), and vanilla extract to the peanut butter mixture. Stir until all the ingredients are evenly distributed and the mixture comes together in a cohesive ball.
3. Scoop out spoonfuls of the mixture and roll them into bite-sized balls using your hands.
4. Place the energy bites on a plate or tray and refrigerate for at least 30 minutes before serving.
5. Enjoy your peanut butter chocolate chip energy bites as a tasty and convenient snack on the go!

Nutrition (per 1 energy bite, 1/15th of the recipe) Calories: 100, Fat: 4g, Carbs: 15g, Protein: 3g

Spicy Roasted Tomato Salad

Prep Time: 15 minutes **Cook time:** 30 minutes **Serving:** 4

Ingredients:
- 1 pint cherry or grape tomatoes
- 1 tablespoon olive oil
- 1/2 teaspoon chili powder
- 1/4 teaspoon cumin
- 1/4 teaspoon salt
- 1/4 teaspoon pepper
- 1/4 teaspoon paprika
- 1 small bunch cilantro, leaves chopped

Directions:
1. Preheat your oven to 400°F (200°C). Line a baking sheet with parchment paper.
2. Place the cherry or grape tomatoes on the prepared baking sheet. Drizzle with olive oil and sprinkle with chili powder, cumin, salt, pepper, and paprika. Toss the tomatoes to evenly coat them with the seasonings.
3. Roast the tomatoes in the preheated oven for 25-30 minutes, or until they are soft and slightly caramelized.
4. Once the tomatoes are finished roasting, transfer them to a large mixing bowl. Add the chopped cilantro leaves to the bowl. Gently toss the ingredients together to combine.
5. Divide the tomato salad among four plates or bowls.

6. Serve immediately and enjoy as a healthy snack.

Nutrition (per serving): Calories: 70, Fat: 5g, Carbs: 7g, Protein: 2g

No-Cook Pistachio-Cranberry Quinoa Bites

Prep Time: 15 minutes **Cook time:** 0 minutes **Serving:** 12-15 bites

Ingredients:
- 1 cup cooked quinoa
- 1/2 cup dried cranberries
- 1/2 cup unsalted, shelled pistachios
- 2 tbsp honey or maple syrup
- 2 tbsp coconut oil, melted
- 1 tsp vanilla extract

Directions:
1. In a medium mixing bowl, combine the cooked quinoa, dried cranberries, and pistachios. Mix until well combined.
2. In a small separate bowl, whisk together the honey or maple syrup, melted coconut oil, and vanilla extract. Pour the mixture over the quinoa mixture and stir until the ingredients are evenly coated.
3. Scoop out spoonfuls of the mixture and roll them into bite-sized balls using your hands.
4. Place the quinoa bites on a plate or tray and refrigerate for at least 30 minutes before serving.
5. Enjoy your no-cook pistachio-cranberry quinoa bites as a healthy and satisfying snack!

Nutrition (per serving): 1 quinoa bite (1/12th of the recipe), Calories: 110, Fat: 7g, Carbs: 13g, Protein: 2g

No-Bake Honey-Almond Granola Bars

Prep Time: 15 minutes **Cook time:** 0 minutes **Serving:** 16 bars

Ingredients:
- 2 cups old-fashioned oats
- 1 cup unsalted, roasted almonds, roughly chopped
- 1/4 cup honey
- 1/4 cup almond butter
- 1/4 cup coconut oil, melted
- 1 tsp vanilla extract
- 1/4 tsp salt

Directions:
1. In a medium mixing bowl, combine the oats and chopped almonds. Mix until well combined.
2. In a small separate bowl, whisk together the honey, almond butter, melted coconut oil, vanilla extract, and salt. Pour the mixture over the oat mixture and stir until the ingredients are evenly coated.
3. Press the mixture into an even layer in an 8x8 inch pan lined with parchment paper.
4. Place the pan in the refrigerator for at least 1 hour before slicing into bars.
5. Enjoy your no-bake honey-almond granola bars as a healthy and convenient snack!

Nutrition (per serving): 1 granola bar (1/16th of the recipe), Calories: 200, Fat: 14g, Carbs: 17g, Protein: 5g

Cottage Cheese-Filled Avocado

Prep Time: 5 minutes **Cook time:** 0 minutes **Serving:** 1

Ingredients:
- 1 avocado
- 1/4 cup cottage cheese
- Salt and pepper, to taste

Directions:
1. Cut the avocado in half and remove the pit. Scoop out some of the avocado flesh from each half, leaving a thicker border around the edge.
2. Fill the avocado halves with the cottage cheese.
3. Sprinkle with salt and pepper to taste.
4. Enjoy your cottage cheese-filled avocado as a tasty and healthy snack or breakfast!

Nutrition (per 1 filled avocado): Calories: 200, Fat: 15g, Carbs: 11g, Protein: 9g

Baked Spinach Chips

Prep Time: 5 minutes **Cook time:** 10 minutes **Serving:** 4

Ingredients:
- 2 cups packed baby spinach
- 2 tbsp olive oil
- Salt, to taste

Directions:
1. Preheat your oven to 350°F (180°C). Line a baking sheet with parchment paper.
2. Place the spinach in a blender or food processor and pulse until it is finely chopped.
3. Transfer the chopped spinach to a mixing bowl and add the olive oil and salt. Stir until the spinach is evenly coated with the oil and seasoning.
4. Spread the spinach mixture in an even layer on the prepared baking sheet.
5. Bake the spinach in the preheated oven for 8-10 minutes, or until it is crispy and lightly browned.
6. Remove the spinach from the oven and let it cool for a few minutes before serving. Enjoy your baked spinach chips as a healthy and tasty snack!

Nutrition (per serving): Calories: 80, Fat: 7g, Carbs: 4g, Protein: 2g

Pumpkin & Banana Waffles

Prep Time: 10 minutes **Cook time:** 10 minutes **Serving:** 4

Ingredients:
- 1/4 cup all-purpose flour
- 1 tsp baking powder
- 1/4 tsp cinnamon
- 1/4 tsp nutmeg
- 1/4 tsp salt
- 1/4 cup unsweetened almond milk
- 1/4 cup pumpkin puree
- 1 egg white
- 1/4 banana, mashed
- 1 tsp olive oil or melted butter

Directions:

1. In a medium mixing bowl, whisk together the flour, baking powder, cinnamon, nutmeg, and salt.
2. In a separate small mixing bowl, whisk together the almond milk, pumpkin puree, egg white, mashed banana, and olive oil or melted butter.
3. Pour the wet mixture into the dry mixture and stir until just combined.
4. Preheat your waffle iron. Lightly grease the waffle iron with cooking spray or melted butter.
5. Pour the waffle batter into the waffle iron and cook according to the manufacturer's instructions, until the waffles are golden brown and crispy. Repeat with the remaining batter.
6. Serve the pumpkin and banana waffles with low calorie syrup, if desired. Enjoy!
   Note: This recipe is Lean&Green compliant when served with a green serving of vegetables on the side.

Nutrition (per 1 waffle, 1/4th of the recipe): Calories: 130, Fat: 5g, Carbs: 17g, Protein: 5g.

Pudding with Chia and Berries

Prep Time: 10 minutes **Cook time:** 0 minutes **Serving:** 1

Ingredients:

- 1/2 cup unsweetened almond milk
- 2 tbsp chia seeds
- 1 tsp Stevia or other zero-calorie sweetener
- 1 tsp vanilla extract
- 1/2 cup mixed berries (such as strawberries, raspberries, and blueberries)

Directions:

1. In a small mixing bowl, whisk together the almond milk, chia seeds, Stevia or other zero-calorie sweetener, and vanilla extract.
2. Divide the mixture evenly among 1 small bowl or glass.
3. Top each bowl with 1/2 cup of mixed berries.
4. Cover and refrigerate the pudding for at least 4 hours or overnight, until it has thickened.
5. Serve the pudding with chia and berries chilled, and enjoy!

Nutrition (per serving, 1 bowl of pudding): Calories: 70, Fat: 4g, Carbs: 8g, Protein: 3g

Swiss Chard and Spinach with Egg

Prep Time: 10 minutes **Cook time:** 10 minutes **Serving:** 4

Ingredients:

- 1 tbsp olive oil
- 1 onion, diced
- 4 cloves garlic, minced
- 1 bunch Swiss chard, stems removed and leaves chopped
- 1 bunch spinach, stems removed and leaves chopped
- 4 large eggs
- Salt and pepper to taste

Directions:

1. Heat the olive oil in a large skillet over medium heat. Add the onion and garlic and cook until softened, about 5 minutes.
2. Add the Swiss chard and spinach to the skillet and cook until wilted, about 5 minutes.

3. Make four wells in the greens and crack an egg into each well. Sprinkle with salt and pepper.
4. Cover the skillet and cook until the eggs are cooked to your desired level of doneness, about 3-5 minutes for over-easy or 5-7 minutes for over-medium.
5. Serve the dish immediately and enjoy!

Nutrition (per serving): Fat: 15g, Protein: 12g, Carbohydrates: 6g, Sodium: 122mg

Greek Yogurt Sticks

Prep Time: 5 minutes **Cook time:** 0 minutes **Serving:** 4

Ingredients:
- 2 cups Greek yogurt
- 1/2 cup granola
- 1 cup mixed berries (such as strawberries, raspberries, and blueberries)

Directions:
1. Line a baking sheet with parchment paper.
2. Using a small cookie scoop or spoon, scoop out small balls of Greek yogurt and place them on the prepared baking sheet. You should get about 16 yogurt balls.
3. Freeze the yogurt balls for at least 2 hours or overnight, until they are firm.
4. Once the yogurt balls are frozen, remove them from the freezer and insert a toothpick or popsicle stick into each one.
5. Roll the yogurt balls in granola to coat them evenly.
6. Serve the Greek yogurt sticks with mixed berries as a healthy and refreshing snack or dessert. Enjoy!

Nutrition (per serving, 4 Greek yogurt sticks, 1/4th of the recipe): Calories: 200, Fat: 7g, Carbs: 26g, Protein: 11g

Cucumber and Feta Stuffed Peppers

Prep Time: 10 minutes **Cook time:** 25 minutes **Serving:** 4

Ingredients:
- 2 bell peppers (red, yellow or green)
- 1 cup of diced cucumber
- 1/4 cup of crumbled feta cheese
- 1/4 cup of diced red onion
- 2 tablespoons of chopped fresh parsley
- 1 tablespoon of lemon juice
- Salt and pepper, to taste

Directions:
1. Preheat the oven to 375°F.
2. Cut the bell peppers in half and remove the seeds.
3. In a small bowl, mix together the diced cucumber, feta cheese, red onion, parsley, lemon juice, salt, and pepper.
4. Stuff the bell pepper halves with the cucumber and feta mixture.
5. Place the stuffed bell peppers in a baking dish and bake for 20-25 minutes, or until the peppers are tender.
6. Serve and enjoy!

Nutrition (per serving): Calories: 66, Protein: 3g, Fat: 4g, Carbohydrates: 5g, Fiber: 1g, Sugar: 3g

Avocado and Tomato Toast

Prep Time: 10 minutes **Cook time:** 25 minutes **Serving:** 4

Ingredients:

- 2 slices of whole wheat bread, toasted
- 1/2 avocado, mashed
- 2-3 cherry tomatoes, diced
- Salt and pepper, to taste
- 1 tablespoon of chopped fresh basil

Directions:

1. Toast the bread slices until golden brown.
2. Spread the mashed avocado on top of the toast slices.
3. Add diced tomatoes on top of the avocado spread.
4. Season with salt and pepper to taste.
5. Sprinkle chopped basil on top.
6. Serve and enjoy!

Nutrition (per serving): Calories: 150, Protein: 4g, Fat: 10g, Carbohydrates: 13g, Fiber: 4g, Sugar: 2g

Chapter 7: Desserts Recipes

Cinnamon Apple Nachos

Prep Time: 5 minutes **Cook time:** 0 minutes **Serving:** 1

Ingredients:
- 1 small apple, thinly sliced
- 1 tsp cinnamon
- 1 tsp honey or agave nectar
- 1 tbsp chopped pecans

Directions:
1. Arrange the apple slices on a plate.
2. Sprinkle the cinnamon over the apple slices.
3. Drizzle the honey or agave nectar over the top.
4. Sprinkle the chopped pecans over the apple slices.
5. Serve and enjoy as a healthy and satisfying dessert.

Nutrition (per serving): Calories: 110, Fat: 4g, Carbs: 19g, Protein: 1g

Strawberry Greek Yogurt Parfait

Prep Time: 10 minutes **Cook time:** 0 minutes **Serving:** 2

Ingredients:
- 1 cup fresh strawberries, diced
- 1 cup plain Greek yogurt
- 2 tablespoons sweetener of choice (such as stevia or erythritol)
- 1/4 cup low-carb granola alternative (such as almond flour or coconut flakes)

Directions:
1. In a medium bowl, mix together the diced strawberries and sweetener of choice.
2. In two parfait glasses or bowls, layer the Greek yogurt and strawberry mixture.
3. Top each parfait with 2 tablespoons of low-carb granola alternative.
4. Serve immediately and enjoy your delicious and healthy Strawberry Yogurt Parfait.

Nutrition (per serving, 1 parfait, 1/2 of the recipe): Calories: 150, Fat: 2g, Carbs: 6g, Protein: 14g

Berry and Yogurt Parfait

Prep Time: 5 minutes **Cook time:** 0 minutes **Serving:** 4

Ingredients:
- 2 cups mixed berries (such as raspberries and blueberries)
- 1 cup plain Greek yogurt
- 1/4 cup honey
- 1/4 cup chopped nuts (such as almonds or walnuts)

Directions:
1. Layer the mixed berries, Greek yogurt, honey, and chopped nuts in four small glasses or parfait cups.
2. Serve the parfait immediately and enjoy!

Nutrition (per serving, 1 parfait, 1/4 of the recipe): Calories: 200, Fat: 7g, Carbs: 25g, Protein: 12g

Fruit and Nut Bites

Prep Time: 10 minutes **Cook time:** 0 minutes **Serving:** 12 bites

Ingredients:
- 1 cup dried apricots
- 1/2 cup dried cranberries
- 1/2 cup raw almonds
- 1/2 cup raw walnuts
- 1/4 cup chia seeds
- 1/4 cup hemp seeds
- 1/4 cup unsweetened shredded coconut
- 1/4 cup honey or agave nectar

Directions:
1. In a food processor, pulse the apricots, cranberries, almonds, and walnuts until they are finely chopped.
2. Add in the chia seeds, hemp seeds, and shredded coconut, and pulse until everything is well combined.
3. Add in the honey or agave nectar and pulse again until the mixture forms a sticky dough.
4. Roll the mixture into small balls, about the size of a cherry.
5. Place the balls on a plate or baking sheet, and refrigerate for at least 30 minutes or until firm.
6. Serve the fruit and nut bites as a healthy and satisfying snack or dessert.

Nutrition (per serving, 1 bite, 1/12th of the recipe), Calories: 150, Fat: 12g, Carbs: 12g, Protein: 3g

Baked Apple Wedges

Prep Time: 10 minutes **Cook time:** 30 minutes **Serving:** 4

Ingredients:
- 4 medium apples, cored and sliced into wedges
- 1/4 cup granulated sugar
- 1 tsp ground cinnamon
- 1/4 tsp nutmeg
- 1 tbsp lemon juice
- 1 tbsp butter or margarine

Directions:
1. Preheat your oven to 375°F (190°C). Grease a baking sheet with cooking spray.
2. In a small mixing bowl, combine the sugar, cinnamon, and nutmeg.
3. In a separate bowl, toss the apple wedges with lemon juice.
4. Dip each apple wedge into the sugar mixture, making sure to coat evenly.
5. Place the coated apple wedges on the prepared baking sheet and dot with butter or margarine.
6. Bake the apples for 25-30 minutes, or until they are tender and golden brown.
7. Remove the apples from the oven and let them cool for a few minutes before serving.
8. Serve the Baked Apple Wedges warm as a healthy and delicious dessert. Enjoy!

Nutrition (per serving, 1/4 of the recipe): Calories: 110, Fat: 3g, Carbs: 25g, Protein: 1g

Berry Sorbet

Prep Time: 10 minutes **Serving:** 6

Ingredients:
- 3 cups mixed berries (such as strawberries, raspberries, and blueberries)
- 1/2 cup granulated sugar
- 1/4 cup lemon juice
- 1 tbsp honey

Directions:
1. In a blender or food processor, puree the berries until smooth.
2. In a small saucepan, combine the sugar, lemon juice, and honey. Heat over medium heat, stirring occasionally, until the sugar has dissolved.
3. Stir the sugar mixture into the pureed berries.
4. Pour the mixture into a shallow dish and place it in the freezer.
5. Every 30 minutes, take the dish out of the freezer and use a fork to scrape the mixture, breaking up any ice crystals that have formed. Repeat this process for about 2-3 hours, or until the sorbet is frozen and smooth.
6. Serve the sorbet in small bowls or glasses, garnished with fresh berries, if desired.

Nutrition (per serving): Calories: 90, Fat: 0g, Carbs: 23g, Protein: 1g

Strawberry Banana Smoothie

Prep Time: 5 minutes **Serving:** 1

Ingredients:
- 1 cup frozen strawberries
- 1 banana
- 1/2 cup Greek yogurt
- 1/2 cup unsweetened almond milk
- 1 tsp erythritol or any other low-carb sweetener (optional)

Directions:
1. Place all ingredients in a blender and blend until smooth.
2. Pour the smoothie into a glass and enjoy immediately.

Nutrition (per serving): Calories: 150 Fat: 3g Carbs: 12g Protein: 11g Sugar: 6g Sodium: 60mg

Tropical Smoothie Bowl

Prep Time: 5 minutes **Cook time:** 0 minutes **Serving:** 1

Ingredients:
- 1 cup frozen strawberries
- 1/2 frozen banana
- 1/2 cup coconut milk
- 1/2 cup unsweetened almond milk
- 1 tsp stevia or any other low-carb sweetener (optional)

Directions:
1. Add all ingredients to a blender.
2. Blend until smooth.

3. Pour into a bowl.
4. Garnish with your favorite tropical fruit and chopped nuts.
5. Serve immediately and enjoy!

Optional toppings:
- Sliced berries
- Sliced avocado
- Chopped nuts
- Shredded coconut

Nutrition (per serving): Calories: 156 Fat: 12g Carbs: 12g Protein: 3g Sodium: 21mg

Chia Seed Pudding

Prep Time: 5 minutes **Cook time:** 4 hours (refrigeration time) **Serving:** 4

Ingredients:
- 1 cup unsweetened almond milk
- 1 cup unsweetened coconut milk
- 1/2 cup chia seeds
- 2 tbsp honey
- 1 tsp vanilla extract
- 1/4 tsp cinnamon (optional)

Directions:
1. In a medium bowl, whisk together the almond milk, coconut milk, honey, vanilla extract, and cinnamon (if using).
2. Add the chia seeds to the mixture and stir well to combine.
3. Cover the bowl with plastic wrap and refrigerate for at least 4 hours or overnight.
4. When ready to serve, give the mixture a stir to redistribute the chia seeds.
5. Divide the pudding into 4 bowls and garnish with your favorite fruit and nuts.
6. Enjoy!

Optional toppings:
- Sliced banana
- Sliced strawberries
- Chopped nuts
- Coconut flakes
- Granola

Nutrition (per serving): Calories: 213 Fat: 13g Carbs: 22g Protein: 7g Sodium: 63mg

Blueberry Cheesecake Muffins

Prep Time: 15 minutes **Cook time:** 20 minutes **Serving:** 12

Ingredients:
- 1 1/2 cups all-purpose flour
- 1 tsp baking powder
- 1/4 tsp salt
- 1/2 cup granulated sugar
- 1/2 cup low-fat cream cheese, softened
- 1 egg
- 1/2 cup unsweetened almond milk

- 1 tsp vanilla extract
- 1 cup fresh blueberries

Directions:

1. Preheat your oven to 350°F (180°C) and line a muffin tin with muffin cups.
2. In a medium mixing bowl, whisk together the flour, baking powder, and salt.
3. In a separate large mixing bowl, beat the cream cheese and sugar together until smooth. Beat in the egg, followed by the almond milk and vanilla extract.
4. Gradually add the dry ingredients to the wet ingredients, mixing until just combined. Gently fold in the blueberries.
5. Spoon the batter into the prepared muffin cups, filling each about 2/3 full.
6. Bake the muffins for 18-20 minutes, or until a toothpick inserted into the center comes out clean.
7. Remove the muffins from the oven and let them cool in the tin for a few minutes before transferring to a wire rack to cool completely.
8. Serve the Blueberry Cheesecake Muffins as a healthy and delicious dessert option. Enjoy!

Nutrition (per serving): Calories: 150, Fat: 4g, Carbs: 25g, Protein: 4g, Sodium: 175mg

Potato Bagels

Prep Time: 45 minutes **Cook time:** 25 minutes **Serving:** 8

Ingredients:

- 2 cups mashed potatoes
- 1/2 cup almond flour
- 1/2 cup coconut flour
- 1 tbsp erythritol or any other low-carb sweetener
- 1 tsp salt
- 2 tsp active dry yeast
- 1 egg, beaten
- Sesame seeds or poppy seeds for topping (optional)

Directions:

1. In a large bowl, combine the mashed potatoes, almond flour, coconut flour, erythritol, salt, and yeast. Mix until a dough forms.
2. On a lightly floured surface, knead the dough for about 10 minutes or until it becomes smooth and elastic.
3. Place the dough in a greased bowl, cover with a towel, and set aside in a warm place to rise for about 30 minutes or until it doubles in size.
4. Preheat your oven to 425°F (220°C). Line a baking sheet with parchment paper.
5. Punch down the dough and divide it into 8 equal pieces. Shape each piece into a round ball and poke a hole through the center with your finger to form a bagel shape.
6. Brush the bagels with the beaten egg and sprinkle with sesame seeds or poppy seeds (if using).
7. Bake the bagels for 25 minutes or until they are golden brown.
8. Remove the bagels from the oven and transfer them to a wire rack to cool.
9. Serve the bagels warm or at room temperature, with your favorite spread or topping. Enjoy!

Nutrition (per serving): Calories: 137 Fat: 10g Carbs: 7g Protein: 7g Sodium: 312mg

No-Bake Chocolate Haystacks

Prep Time: 10 minutes **Cook time:** 0 minutes **Serving:** 24

Ingredients:
- 2 cups crispy rice cereal
- 1/2 cup unsweetened cocoa powder
- 1/2 cup vanilla protein powder
- 1/4 cup almond butter
- 1/4 cup honey

Directions:
1. In a large mixing bowl, combine the cocoa powder, protein powder, almond butter and honey.
2. Add the cereal to the mixture and stir until it is evenly coated.
3. Using a spoon or a cookie scoop, drop spoonfuls of the mixture onto a parchment paper-lined baking sheet.
4. Let the haystacks cool until the chocolate is set.
5. Serve the haystacks as is or roll them in shredded coconut or other toppings (optional). Enjoy!

Nutrition (per serving): Calories: 72 Fat: 3g Carbs: 10g Protein: 4g Sodium: 27mg

Low-Fat Eggnog

Prep Time: 10 minutes **Cook time:** 10 minutes **Serving:** 8

Ingredients:
- 6 large egg whites
- 1/2 cup sugar
- 1/4 tsp salt
- 2 cups skim milk
- 1 cup heavy cream
- 1 tsp vanilla extract
- 1 tsp ground nutmeg
- 1/2 cup dark rum or brandy (optional)

Directions:
1. In a large saucepan, whisk together the egg whites, sugar, and salt.
2. Add the skim milk to the saucepan and place it over medium heat. Cook the mixture, stirring constantly, until it thickens and coats the back of a spoon.
3. Remove the saucepan from the heat and stir in the vanilla extract and nutmeg.
4. If using, stir in the rum or brandy.
5. Pour the eggnog into a large pitcher or punch bowl and refrigerate until chilled.
6. Serve the eggnog cold, garnished with a sprinkle of nutmeg on top. Enjoy!

Optional variations:
- For a non-alcoholic version, omit the rum or brandy.
- For a spicier eggnog, add a pinch of ground cinnamon or a dash of ground cloves to the mixture.

Nutrition (per serving): (based on the use of skim milk and without optional rum or brandy) Calories: 83 Fat: 3g Carbs: 11g Protein: 6g Sodium: 80mg

Modified Marshmallow Cereal Treat

Prep Time: 10 minutes **Cook time:** 10 minutes **Serving:** 12

Ingredients:
- 3 cups whole grain crispy cereal
- 2 cups air-popped popcorn
- 1 cup dried cranberries
- 2 tbsp almond butter
- 1 tsp vanilla extract
- Non-stick cooking spray

Directions:
1. Line a 9x13-inch baking dish with parchment paper or aluminum foil, and lightly coat it with non-stick cooking spray.
2. In a large saucepan, melt the almond butter over medium heat. Stir in the vanilla extract.
3. Remove the saucepan from the heat and stir in the cereal, popcorn, and cranberries.
4. Press the cereal mixture into the prepared baking dish, using a spatula or your hands to evenly distribute it.
5. Let the cereal treats cool completely before cutting them into squares.
6. Serve the cereal treats as is, or top them with chopped nuts or other decorations (optional). Enjoy!

Nutrition (per serving): Calories: 130 Fat: 5g Carbs: 20g Protein: 3g Sodium: 20mg

Chocolate Protein Oat Bars

Prep Time: 15 minutes **Cook time:** 25 minutes **Serving:** 12

Ingredients:
- 1 cup rolled oats
- 1/2 cup whole wheat flour
- 1/2 cup unsweetened cocoa powder
- 1/2 cup vanilla protein powder
- 1/4 tsp baking powder
- 1/4 tsp salt
- 1/2 cup honey
- 1/4 cup unsweetened applesauce
- 1 egg
- 1 tsp vanilla extract

Directions:
1. Preheat the oven to 350°F (175°C) and grease a 9x9 inch baking dish.
2. In a medium bowl, whisk together the oats, flour, cocoa powder, protein powder, baking powder, and salt.
3. In a separate large bowl, mix together the honey, applesauce, egg and vanilla extract.
4. Slowly add the dry ingredients to the wet ingredients and mix until well combined.
5. Spread the mixture into the prepared baking dish and press it down evenly.
6. Bake for 25 minutes or until a toothpick inserted in the center comes out clean.
7. Let the bars cool completely in the baking dish before cutting them into 12 bars.
8. Serve and enjoy!

Nutrition (per serving): Calories: 130 Fat: 2g Carbs: 21g Protein: 7g Sodium: 80mg

Berries and Cream Trifle

Prep Time: 15 minutes **Serving:** 10

Ingredients:
- 4 cups fresh berries (strawberries, blueberries, raspberries)
- 1 cup plain Greek yogurt
- 1/4 cup honey
- 1 tsp vanilla extract
- 1 recipe angel food cake (or 1 store-bought angel food cake), cut into 1-inch cubes

Directions:
1. In a medium bowl, mix together the Greek yogurt, honey, and vanilla extract.
2. Place a layer of angel food cake cubes in the bottom of a trifle dish or large glass bowl.
3. Spread a layer of the yogurt mixture over the cake.
4. Add a layer of mixed berries on top of the yogurt.
5. Repeat layering process until you reach the top of the dish.
6. Top the trifle with whipped cream (if using).
7. Refrigerate for at least 1 hour before serving.

Nutrition (per serving): Calories: 120 Fat: 1g Carbs: 24g Protein: 4g Sodium: 150mg

Coconut Colada Shake

Prep Time: 5 minutes **Cook time:** 0 minutes **Serving:** 1

Ingredients:
- 1 cup coconut milk
- 1/2 cup pineapple juice
- 1/2 cup frozen pineapple chunks
- 1 banana
- 1/4 tsp coconut extract
- 1/2 cup ice
- • 1 cup coconut milk
- • 1/4 cup frozen pineapple chunks
- • 1/2 avocado
- • 1/4 tsp coconut extract
- • 2 tbsp erythritol or any other low-carb sweetener
- • 1/2 cup ice

Directions:
1. Combine all ingredients in a blender.
2. Blend on high until smooth, about 1 minute.
3. Pour the shake into a tall glass and serve immediately.

Nutrition (per serving): Fat: 20g, Net Carbs: 5g, Protein: 2g, Sodium: 35mg

Lean and Green Yogurt Mint

Prep Time: 5 minutes **Cook time:** 0 minutes **Serving:** 4

Ingredients:
- 2 cups non-fat plain Greek yogurt
- 1/2 cup chopped fresh mint leaves

- 1 tbsp honey
- 1 tsp vanilla extract

Directions:
1. In a blender or food processor, combine the yogurt, mint, honey, and vanilla.
2. Blend until smooth.
3. Pour the mixture into a loaf pan or individual serving dishes and freeze for at least 2 hours, or until firm.
4. To serve, let the yogurt mint sit at room temperature for a few minutes to soften, or scoop it out of the pan and serve it immediately. Optional: Top each serving with a sprinkle of chopped mint leaves and a drizzle of honey before serving.

Nutrition (per serving): Calories: 100 Fat: 0g Protein: 18g Carbs: 11g Sugar: 8g Sodium: 75mg

Baked Cinnamon Donuts

Prep Time: 15 minutes **Cook time:** 15 minutes **Serving:** 6

Ingredients:
- 1 cup whole wheat flour
- 1 tsp baking powder
- 1/4 tsp salt
- 1 tsp ground cinnamon
- 1/4 cup granulated sugar
- 1/4 cup unsweetened applesauce
- 1/4 cup almond milk
- 1 large egg
- 1 tsp vanilla extract

Directions:
1. Preheat the oven to 350°F (175°C). Grease a donut pan with cooking spray or butter.
2. In a medium mixing bowl, whisk together the flour, baking powder, salt, and cinnamon.
3. In a separate small bowl, mix together the sugar, applesauce, almond milk, egg and vanilla extract.
4. Pour the wet mixture into the dry mixture and stir until just combined.
5. Transfer the batter to a large plastic bag or a piping bag. Cut off the corner of the bag, then pipe the batter into the prepared donut pan.
6. Bake the donuts for about 15 minutes, or until a toothpick inserted into the center comes out clean.
7. Allow the donuts to cool in the pan for about 5 minutes, then transfer them to a wire rack to cool completely.
8. Serve the donuts warm or at room temperature. Enjoy!

Nutrition (per serving): Calories: 119kcal, Fat: 2g, Saturated Fat: 0g, Cholesterol: 29mg, Sodium: 116mg, Potassium: 74mg, Carbohydrates: 22g, Fiber: 2g, Sugar: 8g, Protein: 4g

Blueberry Lemon Cheesecake Bars

Prep Time: 10 minutes **Cook time:** 20 minutes **Serving:** 12

Ingredients:
- 1 cup graham cracker crumbs

- 1/4 cup granulated sugar
- 1/2 cup unsalted butter, melted
- 1 (8 oz) package cream cheese, softened
- 1/2 cup granulated sugar
- 1 large egg
- 1/4 cup fresh lemon juice
- 1/2 tsp lemon zest
- 1 cup fresh blueberries

Directions:
1. Preheat your oven to 350°F (175°C). Line a 9x9 inch square baking pan with parchment paper or aluminum foil.
2. In a medium mixing bowl, combine the graham cracker crumbs, 1/4 cup sugar, and melted butter. Press the mixture evenly into the bottom of the prepared pan.
3. In a large mixing bowl, beat the cream cheese and 1/2 cup sugar together until smooth. Add in the egg, lemon juice and lemon zest, and mix until well combined.
4. Spread the cream cheese mixture over the crust, then top with blueberries.
5. Bake for about 20-25 minutes, or until the edges are lightly golden. Remove the cheesecake bars from the oven and let them cool completely.
6. Chill the cheesecake bars in the refrigerator for at least 2 hours before slicing and serving.

Nutrition (per serving): Fat: 17g, Net Carbs: 20g, Protein: 4g, Sodium: 100mg

Skinny Peppermint Mocha

Prep Time: 5 minutes **Cook time:** 5 minutes **Serving:** 1

Ingredients:
- Brewed coffee
- 1 cup Unsweetened almond milk
- 1 cup Peppermint extract
- 1/4 teaspoon Honey or agave nectar
- 1 tablespoon Unsweetened cocoa powder
- 1 tablespoon Whipped cream, for serving (optional)

Directions:
1. In a small saucepan over medium heat, combine the brewed coffee, almond milk, peppermint extract, honey or agave, and cocoa powder.
2. Whisk the mixture continuously until it is well combined and heated through.
3. Pour the mocha into a mug and top with whipped cream, if desired.
4. Savor the pepperminty goodness as you sip on your Skinny Peppermint Mocha.

Nutrition (per serving): Fat: 1g, Net Carbs: 20g, Protein: 4g, Sodium: 84mg (based on using honey and unsweetened almond milk)

Low Carb Strawberry Cheesecake Bites

Prep Time: 20 minutes **Cook time:** 0 minutes **Serving:** 8

Ingredients:
- 8 oz Low-fat cream cheese, softened
- 1/4 cup Granulated erythritol or stevia

- 1 tsp Vanilla extract
- 1 cup Mixed berries (strawberries, blueberries, raspberries)
- 1/4 cup Almond flour
- 1/4 cup Coconut flour
- 1/4 cup Unsalted butter, melted

Directions:
1. n a large mixing bowl, beat the low-fat cream cheese, erythritol or stevia, and vanilla extract until well combined.
2. Fold in the mixed berries.
3. In a separate small bowl, mix together the almond flour, coconut flour, and melted butter.
4. Add the dry ingredients to the cream cheese mixture and stir until well combined.
5. Form the mixture into small balls and place on a lined baking sheet.
6. Freeze for at least 1 hour or until firm.
7. Remove from the freezer and enjoy!

Nutrition (per serving): Fat: 10g, Net Carbs: 5g, Protein: 4g, Sodium: 131mg (Note: These nutritional values are based on using low-fat cream cheese and erythritol, and may vary slightly depending on the sweetener used)

5&1 Meal Plan

WEEK 1

Monday
Fueling 1: Mushroom Spinach Egg Muffins
Fueling 2: Pancake Cinnamon Buns
Fueling 3: Spinach and Feta Omelette
Fueling 4: Three-Bean Medley
Fueling 5: Cinnamon Apple Nachos
L&G Meal: Grilled Tilapia with Lemon Herb Marinade

Tuesday
Fueling 1: Egg Muffin
Fueling 2: Pineapple Mango Pancakes
Fueling 3: Cilantro Lime Yogurt Dip with Veggie Sticks
Fueling 4: Greek Style Mini Burger Pies
Fueling 5: Spicy Zucchini Soup
L&G Meal: Grilled Chicken and Vegetable Paella

Wednesday
Fueling 1: Gingerbread Oatmeal Breakfast
Fueling 2: Peanut Butter and Cottage Cheese Dip
Fueling 3: Grilled Veggie Kabobs
Fueling 4: Crispy Pork Cutlets
Fueling 5: Baked Apple Wedges
L&G Meal: Chicken Kohlrabi Noodles Soup

Thursday
Fueling 1: Flaxseed Porridge with Cinnamon
Fueling 2: Curry Roasted Cauliflower Soup
Fueling 3: Low-Fat Eggnog
Fueling 4: No-Bake Chocolate Haystacks
Fueling 5: Radish Chips
L&G Meal: Feta Lamb Patties

Friday
Fueling 1: Avocado Toast with Radish
Fueling 2: Apple Strawberry Salad
Fueling 3: Broccoli Blue Cheese
Fueling 4: Grilled Peach and Arugula Salad
Fueling 5: Baked Cinnamon Donuts
L&G Meal: Savory Salmon with Cilantro

Saturday
Fueling 1: Cheese Almond Pancakes
Fueling 2: High-Protein Salad
Fueling 3: Greek Style Mini Burger Pies
Fueling 4: Ratatouille
Fueling 5: Skinny Peppermint Mocha
L&G Meal: Marinara Shrimp Zoodles

Sunday
Fueling 1: Healthy Waffles
Fueling 2: Vegetable and Lentil Soup
Fueling 3: Baked Turkey Patties
Fueling 4: Spicy Roasted Tomato Salad
Fueling 5: Blueberry Lemon Cheesecake Bars
L&G Meal: Jalapeno Grilled Salmon with Tomato Confit

WEEK 2

Monday
Fueling 1: Cold Banana Breakfast
Fueling 2: Low Carb Strawberry Cheesecake Bites
Fueling 3: No-Bake Chocolate Haystacks
Fueling 4: Cucumber Salad
Fueling 5: Berry Sorbet
L&G Meal: Parmesan Meatballs with Collard Greens

Tuesday
Fueling 1: Cinnamon Pancakes with Coconut
Fueling 2: Cilantro Lime Yogurt Dip with Veggie Sticks
Fueling 3: Vegetable Hash with White Beans
Fueling 4: Grilled Peach and Arugula Salad
Fueling 5: Lemon Butter Shrimp with Broccoli
L&G Meal: Pumpkin and White Bean Soup with Sage

Wednesday
Fueling 1: Baked Eggs
Fueling 2: Pineapple Mango Pancakes
Fueling 3: Ratatouille
Fueling 4: Tofu Power Bowl
Fueling 5: Mushroom and Spinach Soup
L&G Meal: Chicken Meatballs and Napa Cabbage in Ginger Broth

Thursday
Fueling 1: Protein Muffins
Fueling 2: Chocolate Protein Oat Bars
Fueling 3: Cucumber Salad
Fueling 4: Crispy Pork Cutlets
Fueling 5: Potato Bagels
L&G Meal: Shredded Beef Stew

Friday
Fueling 1: Banana Cashew Toast
Fueling 2: Cold Tomato Summer Vegetable
Soup
Fueling 3: Lemon Butter Shrimp with Broccoli
Fueling 4: Greek Style Mini Burger Pies
Fueling 5: Blueberry Cheesecake Muffins
L&G Meal: Beef Korma

Saturday
Fueling 1: Peanut Butter Yogurt Dip with Fruit
Fueling 2: Vegetable and Lentil Soups
Fueling 3: Spicy Roasted Tomato Salad
Fueling 4: No-Bake Chocolate Haystacks
Fueling 5: Baked Turkey Patties
L&G Meal: Grilled Lime & Garlic Shrimp Salad

Sunday
Fueling 1: Strawberry Yogurt Treat
Fueling 2: Curry Roasted Cauliflower Soup
Fueling 3: Tofu Power Bowl
Fueling 4: Grilled Peach and Arugula Salad
Fueling 5: Coconut Colada Shake
L&G Meal: Mediterranean Chicken and
Vegetables

WEEK 3

Monday
Fueling 1: Apple Oatmeal
Fueling 2: Baked Turkey Patties
Fueling 3: Three-Bean Medley
Fueling 4: No-Bake Chocolate Haystacks
Fueling 5: Mushroom Spinach Egg Muffins
L&G Meal: Chicken Caesar Salad

Tuesday
Fueling 1: Egg Avocado Toast

Fueling 2: Pineapple Mango Pancakes
Fueling 3: Greek Style Mini Burger Pies
Fueling 4: Grilled Peach and Arugula Salad
Fueling 5: Baked Apple Wedges
L&G Meal: Chicken Kohlrabi Noodles Soup

Wednesday
Fueling 1: Mushroom Spinach Egg Muffins
Fueling 2: Low-Fat Eggnog
Fueling 3: Grilled Peach and Arugula Salad
Fueling 4: Ratatouille
Fueling 5: Spicy Zucchini Soup
L&G Meal: Scallops and Sweet Potatoes

Thursday
Fueling 1: Chocolate Chip Cakes
Fueling 2: Blueberry Cheesecake Muffins
Fueling 3: No-Bake Chocolate Haystacks
Fueling 4: Spicy Roasted Tomato Salad
Fueling 5: Black Bean Soup
L&G Meal: Chipotle Chicken and Cauliflower
Rice Bowls

Friday
Fueling 1: Lean and Green Yogurt Mint
Fueling 2: Potato Bagels
Fueling 4: Lemon Butter Shrimp with Broccoli
Fueling 3: Alkaline Carrot and Mushroom Soup
Fueling 5: Apple Strawberry Salad
L&G Meal: Middle Eastern Salmon with
Tomatoes and Cucumber

Saturday
Fueling 1: Cinnamon Apple Nachos
Fueling 2: Berry Sorbet
Fueling 3: Spinach and Feta Omelette
Fueling 4: Cucumber Salad
Fueling 5: Lean Green Cauliflower Soup
L&G Meal: Thai Curry Shrimp

Sunday
Fueling 1: Chocolate Cake with Peanut Butter
Filling or Cream Cheese Icing
Fueling 2: Coconut Colada Shake
Fueling 3: Spicy Roasted Tomato Salad
Fueling 4: Tofu Power Bowl
Fueling 5: Vegetable and Lentil Soup

L&G Meal: Sheet Pan Chicken Fajita Lettuce Wraps

WEEK 4

Monday
Fueling 1: Gingerbread Oatmeal Breakfast
Fueling 2: Pancake Cinnamon Buns
Fueling 3: Cucumber Salad
Fueling 4: Ratatouille
Fueling 5: Crispy Pork Cutlets
L&G Meal: Cabbage Wrapped Beef Pot Stickers

Tuesday
Fueling 1: Flaxseed Porridge with Cinnamon
Fueling 2: Cilantro Lime Yogurt Dip with Veggie Sticks
Fueling 3: Lemon Butter Shrimp with Broccoli
Fueling 4: Greek Style Mini Burger Pies
Fueling 5: Low-Fat Eggnog
L&G Meal: Chicken Meatballs and Napa Cabbage in Ginger Broth

Wednesday
Fueling 1: Avocado Toast with Radish
Fueling 2: Pineapple Mango Pancakes
Fueling 3: Tofu Power Bowl
Fueling 4: Grilled Veggie Kabobs
Fueling 5: Baked Apple Wedges
L&G Meal: Baked Cod with Tomato and Feta Salad

Thursday
Fueling 1: Cheese Almond Pancakes
Fueling 2: Curry Roasted Cauliflower Soup
Fueling 3: Greek Style Mini Burger Pies
Fueling 4: Low-Fat Eggnog
Fueling 5: Blueberry Cheesecake Muffins
L&G Meal: Roast Beef

Friday
Fueling 1: Healthy Waffles
Fueling 2: Baked Cinnamon Donuts
Fueling 3: Baked Turkey Patties
Fueling 4: Broccoli Blue Cheese
Fueling 5: Potato Bagels

L&G Meal: Grilled Salmon with Cucumber Dill Sauce

Saturday
Fueling 1: Cold Banana Breakfast
Fueling 2: Skinny Peppermint Mocha
Fueling 3: No-Bake Chocolate Haystacks
Fueling 4: Greek Style Mini Burger Pies
Fueling 5: Alkaline Carrot and Mushroom Soup
L&G Meal: Sushi Salad

Sunday
Fueling 1: Cinnamon Pancakes with Coconut
Fueling 2: Blueberry Lemon Cheesecake Bars
Fueling 3: Grilled Peach and Arugula Salad
Fueling 4: Coconut Colada Shake
Fueling 5: Berry Sorbet
L&G Meal: Healthy Minestrone Soup

4&2&1 Meal Plan

WEEK 1

Monday
Fueling 1: Mushroom Spinach Egg Muffins
Fueling 2: Pancake Cinnamon Buns
Fueling 3: Cucumber Salad
Fueling 4: Cinnamon Apple Nachos
L&G Meal 1: Grilled Chicken and Vegetable Paella
L&G Meal 2: Beef Ribeye Steak
Snack: Pumpkin Protein Balls

Tuesday
Fueling 1: Gingerbread Oatmeal Breakfast
Fueling 2: Pineapple Mango Pancakes
Fueling 3: Spicy Roasted Tomato Salad
Fueling 4: Spicy Zucchini Soup
L&G Meal 1: Grilled Tilapia with Lemon Herb Marinade
L&G Meal 2: Egg with Dill, Pepper, and Salmon
Snack: Snickerdoodle Pecans

Wednesday
Fueling 1: Egg Muffin
Fueling 2: Low Carb Strawberry Cheesecake Bites
Fueling 3: Grilled Veggie Kabobs
Fueling 4: Berry Sorbet
L&G Meal 1: Chicken Kohlrabi Noodles Soup
L&G Meal 2: Baked Cod with Tomato and Feta Salad
Snack: Peanut Butter Energy Bites

Thursday
Fueling 1: Flaxseed Porridge with Cinnamon
Fueling 2: Curry Roasted Cauliflower Soup
Fueling 3: Low-Fat Eggnog
Fueling 4: Radish Chips
L&G Meal 1: Feta Lamb Patties
L&G Meal 2: Slow Cooked Lentil Soup
Snack: Cottage Cheese-Filled Avocado

Friday
Fueling 1: Avocado Toast with Radish
Fueling 2: Apple Strawberry Salad
Fueling 3: Grilled Peach and Arugula Salad
Fueling 4: Baked Cinnamon Donuts
L&G Meal: Savory Salmon with Cilantro
L&G Meal 2: Tuna & Egg Salad
Snack: Spiced Popcorn

Saturday
Fueling 1: Cheese Almond Pancakes
Fueling 2: Herbed Garlic Black Beans
Fueling 3: Broccoli Blue Cheese
Fueling 4: Skinny Peppermint Mocha
L&G Meal 1: Marinara Shrimp Zoodles
L&G Meal 2: Greek Style Mini Burger Pies
Snack: Baked Spinach Chips

Sunday
Fueling 1: Healthy Waffles
Fueling 2: Vegetable and Lentil Soup
Fueling 3: Alkaline Carrot and Mushroom Soup
Fueling 4: Blueberry Lemon Cheesecake Bars
L&G Meal 1: Jalapeno Grilled Salmon with Tomato Confit
L&G Meal 2: Herb Ground Beef
Snack: Pumpkin & Banana Waffles

WEEK 2

Monday
Fueling 1: Cold Banana Breakfast
Fueling 2: Pineapple Mango Pancakes
Fueling 3: No-Bake Chocolate Haystacks
Fueling 4: Grilled Cauliflower Steaks
L&G Meal 1: Lemon Garlic Oregano Chicken with Asparagus
L&G Meal 2: Baked Cod with Tomato and Feta Salad
Snack: Pudding with Chia and Berries

Tuesday
Fueling 1: Cinnamon Pancakes with Coconut
Fueling 2: Peanut Butter and Cottage Cheese Dip
Fueling 3: Cucumber Salad
Fueling 4: Grilled Peach and Arugula Salad

L&G Meal 1: Pumpkin and White Bean Soup with Sage
L&G Meal 2: Beef Ribeye Steak
Snack: No-Bake Honey-Almond Granola Bars

Wednesday
Fueling 1: Baked Eggs
Fueling 2: Mushroom and Spinach Soup
Fueling 3: Stewed Herbed Fruit
Fueling 4: Baked Apple Wedges
L&G Meal 1: Chicken Meatballs and Napa Cabbage in Ginger Broth
L&G Meal 2: Tuna & Egg Salad
Snack: Snickerdoodle Pecans

Thursday
Fueling 1: Protein Muffins
Fueling 2: Chocolate Protein Oat Bars
Fueling 3: Apple Strawberry Salad
Fueling 4: Potato Bagels
L&G Meal 1: Shredded Beef Stew
L&G Meal 2: Egg with Dill, Pepper, and Salmon
Snack: No-Cook Pistachio-Cranberry Quinoa Bites

Friday
Fueling 1: Banana Cashew Toast
Fueling 2: Grilled Cauliflower Steaks
Fueling 3: Spicy Roasted Tomato Salad
Fueling 4: Blueberry Cheesecake Muffins
L&G Meal 1: Beef Korma
L&G Meal 2: Italian Chicken and Vegetable Soup
Snack: Almond-Stuffed Dates

Saturday
Fueling 1: Peanut Butter Yogurt Dip with Fruit
Fueling 2: Vegetable and Lentil Soups
Fueling 3: Lemon Butter Shrimp with Broccoli
Fueling 4: No-Bake Chocolate Haystacks
L&G Meal 1: Grilled Lime & Garlic Shrimp Salad
L&G Meal 2: Herb Ground Beef
Snack: Swiss Chard and Spinach with Egg

Sunday
Fueling 1: Strawberry Yogurt Treat
Fueling 2: High-Protein Salad

Fueling 3: Grilled Peach and Arugula Salad
Fueling 4: Coconut Colada Shake
L&G Meal 1: Mediterranean Chicken and Vegetables
L&G Meal 2: Slow Cooked Lentil Soup
Snack: Peanut Butter Energy Bites

WEEK 3

Monday
Fueling 1: Apple Oatmeal
Fueling 2: Pancake Cinnamon Buns
Fueling 3: No-Bake Chocolate Haystacks
Fueling 4: Mushroom Spinach Egg Muffins
L&G Meal 1: Chicken Caesar Salad
L&G Meal 2: Meatball Soup
Snack: Pumpkin Protein Balls

Tuesday
Fueling 1: Mushroom Spinach Egg Muffins
Fueling 2: Pineapple Mango Pancakes
Fueling 3: Grilled Peach and Arugula Salad
Fueling 4: Low-Fat Eggnog
L&G Meal 1: Chicken Kohlrabi Noodles Soup
L&G Meal 2: Egg with Dill, Pepper, and Salmon
Snack: Spicy Roasted Tomato Salad

Wednesday
Fueling 1: Egg Avocado Toast
Fueling 2: Baked Apple Wedges
Fueling 3: No-Bake Chocolate Haystacks
Fueling 4: Cucumber Salad
L&G Meal 1: Scallops and Sweet Potatoes
L&G Meal 2: Beef Ribeye Steak
Snack: Spiced Popcorn

Thursday
Fueling 1: Chocolate Chip Cakes
Fueling 2: Blueberry Cheesecake Muffins
Fueling 3: Cilantro Lime Yogurt Dip
Fueling 4: Black Bean Soup
L&G Meal 1: Chipotle Chicken and Cauliflower Rice Bowls
L&G Meal 2: Baked Cod with Tomato and Feta Salad
Snack: Snickerdoodle Pecans

Friday
Fueling 1: Lean and Green Yogurt Mint
Fueling 2: Potato Bagels
Fueling 3: Grilled Peach and Arugula Salad
Fueling 4: Grilled Cauliflower Steaks
L&G Meal: Middle Eastern Salmon with Tomatoes and Cucumber
L&G Meal 2: Tuna & Egg Salad
Snack: No-Cook Pistachio-Cranberry Quinoa Bites

Saturday
Fueling 1: Cinnamon Apple Nachos
Fueling 2: Alkaline Carrot and Mushroom Soup
Fueling 3: Herbed Garlic Black Beans
Fueling 4: Radish Chips
L&G Meal 1: Thai Curry Shrimp
L&G Meal 2: Slow Cooked Lentil Soup
Snack: Easy Chicken Curry

Sunday
Fueling 1: Egg Muffin
Fueling 2: No-Bake Chocolate Haystacks
Fueling 3: Spicy Roasted Tomato Salad
Fueling 4: Vegetable and Lentil Soup
L&G Meal 1: Sheet Pan Chicken Fajita Lettuce Wraps
L&G Meal 2: Herb Ground Beef
Snack: Cottage Cheese-Filled Avocado

WEEK 4

Monday
Fueling 1: Gingerbread Oatmeal Breakfast
Fueling 2: Pancake Cinnamon Buns
Fueling 3: Spinach and Feta Omelette
Fueling 4: Berry Sorbet
L&G Meal 1: Cabbage Wrapped Beef Pot Stickers
L&G Meal 2: Italian Chicken and Vegetable Soup
Snack: Spicy Roasted Tomato Salad

Tuesday
Fueling 1: Flaxseed Porridge with Cinnamon
Fueling 2: Cilantro Lime Yogurt Dip with Veggie Sticks

Fueling 3: Lemon Butter Shrimp with Broccoli
Fueling 4: Low-Fat Eggnog
L&G Meal 1: Chicken Meatballs and Napa Cabbage in Ginger Broth
L&G Meal 2: Greek Style Mini Burger Pies
Snack: No-Cook Pistachio-Cranberry Quinoa Bites

Wednesday
Fueling 1: Avocado Toast with Radish
Fueling 2: Pineapple Mango Pancakes
Fueling 3: Grilled Veggie Kabobs
Fueling 4: Baked Apple Wedges
L&G Meal 1: Baked Cod with Tomato and Feta Salad
L&G Meal 2: Roasted Zucchini Boats with Ground Beef
Snack: Baked Spinach Chips

Thursday
Fueling 1: Cheese Almond Pancakes
Fueling 2: Curry Roasted Cauliflower Soup
Fueling 3: Greek Style Mini Burger Pies
Fueling 4: Low-Fat Eggnog
L&G Meal 1: Roast Beef
L&G Meal 2: Meatball Soup
Snack: Pumpkin & Banana Waffles

Friday
Fueling 1: Healthy Waffles
Fueling 2: Chilled Avocado Tomato Soup
Fueling 3: Broccoli Blue Cheese
Fueling 4: Potato Bagels
L&G Meal 1: Grilled Salmon with Cucumber Dill Sauce
L&G Meal 2: Beef Ribeye Steak
Snack: Snickerdoodle Pecans

Saturday
Fueling 1: Cold Banana Breakfast
Fueling 2: Skinny Peppermint Mocha
Fueling 4: Berries and Cream Trifle
Fueling 5: High-Protein Salad
L&G Meal 1: Feta Lamb Patties
L&G Meal 2: Egg with Dill, Pepper, and Salmon
Snack: Peanut Butter Energy Bites

3&3 Meal Plan

WEEK 1

Monday
Fueling 1: Peanut Butter Yogurt Dip with Fruit
Fueling 2: Roasted Zucchini Boats with Ground Beef
Fueling 3: Cinnamon Apple Nachos
L&G Meal 1: Crispy Pork Cutlets
L&G Meal 2: Scallops and Sweet Potatoes
L&G Meal 3: Black Bean Soup

Tuesday
Fueling 1: Mushroom Spinach Egg Muffins
Fueling 2: Pumpkin Protein Balls
Fueling 3: Strawberry Greek Yogurt Parfait
L&G Meal 1: Herb Ground Beef
L&G Meal 2: Salmon and Shrimp Salad
L&G Meal 3: Vegetable and Lentil Soup

Wednesday
Fueling 1: Egg Muffin
Fueling 2: Easy Chicken Curry
Fueling 3: Berry and Yogurt Parfait
L&G Meal 1: Roasted Sirloin Steak
L&G Meal 2: Shrimp, Tomato and Dates Salad
L&G Meal 3: Broccoli Blue Cheese

Thursday
Fueling 1: Baked Eggs
Fueling 2: Spiced Popcorn
Fueling 3: Fruit and Nut Bites
L&G Meal 1: Baked Turkey Patties
L&G Meal 2: Salmon and Watercress Salad
L&G Meal 3: Mushroom and Spinach Soup

Friday
Fueling 1: Egg Avocado Toast
Fueling 2: Snickerdoodle Pecans
Fueling 3: Baked Apple Wedges
L&G Meal 1: Beef Patties
L&G Meal 2: Savory Salmon with Cilantro
L&G Meal 3: Cold Cauliflower-Coconut Soup

Saturday
Fueling 1: Gingerbread Oatmeal Breakfast
Fueling 2: Almond-Stuffed Date
Fueling 3: Berry Sorbet
L&G Meal 1: Feta Lamb Patties
L&G Meal 2: Middle Eastern Salmon with Tomatoes and Cucumber
L&G Meal 3: Cream of Broccoli & Cauliflower Soup

Sunday
Fueling 1: Avocado Toast with Radish
Fueling 2: Peanut Butter Energy Bites
Fueling 3: Strawberry Banana Smoothie
L&G Meal 1: Grilled Chicken Stroganoff
L&G Meal 2: Grilled Salmon with Spinach and Parmesan
L&G Meal 3: Cold Tomato Summer Vegetable Soup

WEEK 2

Monday
Fueling 1: Cheese Almond Pancakes
Fueling 2: Spicy Roasted Tomato Salad
Fueling 3: Tropical Smoothie Bowl
L&G Meal 1: Beef Ribeye Steak
L&G Meal 2: Grilled Tilapia with Lemon Herb Marinade
L&G Meal 3: Spinach and Coconut Milk Soup

Tuesday
Fueling 1: Healthy Waffles
Fueling 2: No-Cook Pistachio-Cranberry Quinoa Bites
Fueling 3: Chia Seed Pudding
L&G Meal 1: Roast Beef
L&G Meal 2: Thai Curry Shrimp
L&G Meal 3: Alkaline Carrot and Mushroom Soup

Wednesday
Fueling 1: Protein Muffins
Fueling 2: No-Bake Honey-Almond Granola Bars

Fueling 3: Blueberry Cheesecake Muffins
L&G Meal 1: Beef Korma
L&G Meal 2: Tuna & Egg Salad
L&G Meal 3: Lean Green Cauliflower Soup

Thursday
Fueling 1: Cold Banana Breakfast
Fueling 2: Cottage Cheese-Filled Avocado
Fueling 3: Potato Bagels
L&G Meal 1: Sheet Pan Chicken Fajita Lettuce Wraps
L&G Meal 2: Garlic Lemon Shrimp
L&G Meal 3: Chilled Avocado Tomato Soup

Friday
Fueling 1: Strawberry Yogurt Treat
Fueling 2: Baked Spinach Chips
Fueling 3: No-Bake Chocolate Haystacks
L&G Meal 1: Lemon Garlic Oregano Chicken with Asparagus
L&G Meal 2: Sushi Salad
L&G Meal 3: Pumpkin and White Bean Soup with Sage

Saturday
Fueling 1: Apple Oatmeal
Fueling 2: Pumpkin & Banana Waffles
Fueling 3: Low-Fat Eggnog
L&G Meal 1: Chipotle Chicken and Cauliflower Rice Bowls
L&G Meal 2: Marinara Shrimp Zoodles
L&G Meal 3: Italian Chicken and Vegetable Soup

Sunday
Fueling 1: Banana Cashew Toast
Fueling 2: Pudding with Chia and Berries
Fueling 3: Modified Marshmallow Cereal Treat
L&G Meal 1: Chicken Caesar Salad
L&G Meal 2: Grilled Lime & Garlic Shrimp Salad
L&G Meal 3: Slow Cooked Lentil Soup

WEEK 3

Monday
Fueling 1: Cinnamon Pancakes with Coconut
Fueling 2: Swiss Chard and Spinach with Egg

Fueling 3: Chocolate Protein Oat Bars
L&G Meal 1: Mediterranean Chicken and Vegetables
L&G Meal 2: Grilled Lemon and Herb Salmon
L&G Meal 3: Healthy Minestrone Soup

Tuesday
Fueling 1: Flaxseed Porridge with Cinnamon
Fueling 2: Greek Yogurt Sticks
Fueling 3: Berries and Cream Trifle
L&G Meal 1: Shredded Beef Stew
L&G Meal 2: Grilled Salmon with Cucumber Dill Sauce
L&G Meal 3: Chicken Kohlrabi Noodles Soup

Wednesday
Fueling 1: Pancake Cinnamon Buns
Fueling 2: Cucumber and Feta Stuffed Peppers
Fueling 3: Coconut Colada Shake
L&G Meal 1: Grilled Chicken and Vegetable Paella
L&G Meal 2: Jalapeno Grilled Salmon with Tomato Confit
L&G Meal 3: Curry Roasted Cauliflower Soup

Thursday
Fueling 1: Pineapple Mango Pancakes
Fueling 2: Avocado and Tomato Toast
Fueling 3: Lean and Green Yogurt Mint
L&G Meal 1: Chicken Meatballs and Napa Cabbage in Ginger Broth
L&G Meal 2: Egg with Dill, Pepper, and Salmon
L&G Meal 3: Spicy Zucchini Soup

Friday
Fueling 1: Chocolate Cake with Peanut Butter Filling
Fueling 2: Roasted Zucchini Boats with Ground Beef
Fueling 3: Baked Cinnamon Donuts
L&G Meal 1: Parmesan Meatballs with Collard Greens
L&G Meal 2: Lemon Butter Shrimp with Broccoli
L&G Meal 3: Egg Drop Soup

Saturday

Fueling 1: Chocolate Chip Cakes
Fueling 2: Pumpkin Protein Balls
Fueling 3: Blueberry Lemon Cheesecake Bars
L&G Meal 1: Lean and Green Grilled Chicken
L&G Meal 2: Baked Cod with Tomato and Feta Salad
L&G Meal 3: Meatball Soup

Sunday
Fueling 1: Breakfast Scramble
Fueling 2: Easy Chicken Curry
Fueling 3: Skinny Peppermint Mocha
L&G Meal 1: Turkey and Vegetable Stir-Fry
L&G Meal 2: Grilled Salmon with Vegetable Medley
L&G Meal 3: Spinach and Lentil Soup

WEEK 4

Monday
Fueling 1: Breakfast Smoothie
Fueling 2: Spiced Popcorn
Fueling 3: Low Carb Strawberry Cheesecake Bites
L&G Meal 1: Crispy Pork Cutlets
L&G Meal 2: Scallops and Sweet Potatoes
L&G Meal 3: Broccoli and Cheddar Soup

Tuesday
Fueling 1: Breakfast Wrap
Fueling 2: Snickerdoodle Pecans
Fueling 3: Cinnamon Apple Nachos
L&G Meal 1: Herb Ground Beef
L&G Meal 2: Salmon and Shrimp Salad
L&G Meal 3: Black Bean Soup

Wednesday
Fueling 1: Peanut Butter Yogurt Dip with Fruit
Fueling 2: Almond-Stuffed Dates
Fueling 3: Strawberry Greek Yogurt Parfait
L&G Meal 1: Roasted Sirloin Steak
L&G Meal 2: Shrimp, Tomato and Dates Salad
L&G Meal 3: Vegetable and Lentil Soup

Thursday
Fueling 1: Mushroom Spinach Egg Muffins
Fueling 2: Peanut Butter Energy Bites

Fueling 3: Berry and Yogurt Parfait
L&G Meal 1: Baked Turkey Patties
L&G Meal 2: Salmon and Watercress Salad
L&G Meal 3: Broccoli Blue Cheese

Friday
Fueling 1: Egg Muffin
Fueling 2: Spicy Roasted Tomato Salad
Fueling 3: Fruit and Nut Bites
L&G Meal 1: Beef Patties
L&G Meal 2: Savory Salmon with Cilantro
L&G Meal 3: Mushroom and Spinach Sou

Saturday
Fueling 1: Baked Eggs
Fueling 2: No-Cook Pistachio-Cranberry Quinoa Bites
Fueling 3: Baked Apple Wedges
L&G Meal 1: Feta Lamb Patties
L&G Meal 2: Middle Eastern Salmon with Tomatoes and Cucumber
L&G Meal 3: Cold Cauliflower-Coconut Soup

Sunday
Fueling 1: Egg Avocado Toast
Fueling 2: No-Bake Honey-Almond Granola Bars
Fueling 3: Berry Sorbet
L&G Meal 1: Grilled Chicken Stroganoff
L&G Meal 2: Grilled Salmon with Spinach and Parmesan
L&G Meal 3: Cream of Broccoli & Cauliflower Soup